The Majestic Place

The Majestic Place

The Freedom Possible in Black Women's Leadership

Edited by
Wendi S. Williams, PhD
Whitneé L. Garrett-Walker, EdD

Associate Editor
Nia Spooner

ROWMAN & LITTLEFIELD
Lanham • Boulder • New York • London

Published by Rowman & Littlefield
An imprint of The Rowman & Littlefield Publishing Group, Inc.
4501 Forbes Boulevard, Suite 200, Lanham, Maryland 20706
www.rowman.com

86-90 Paul Street, London EC2A 4NE

Copyright © 2025 by The Rowman & Littlefield Publishing Group, Inc.

All rights reserved. No part of this book may be reproduced in any form or by any electronic or mechanical means, including information storage and retrieval systems, without written permission from the publisher, except by a reviewer who may quote passages in a review.

British Library Cataloguing in Publication Information available

Library of Congress Cataloging-in-Publication Data available

ISBN: 978-1-5381-9858-2 (cloth)
ISBN: 978-1-5381-9859-9 (paperback)
ISBN: 978-1-5381-9860-5 (ebook)

Contents

Introduction: You Are Welcome   vii
Wendi Williams, Whitneé Garrett-Walker, and Nia Spooner

PART I: MOTHER'S MILK   1
Whitneé Garrett-Walker

1. I Never Wanted to Be a Midwife: Stories of Birth   3
   Kaiayo Z. Shatteen

2. *Dando LECHE:* Conceptualizing Black-Centered Leadership as Mothering Through the *Testimonios* of Two AfroLatinx Higher Education Professionals   15
   Krista L. Cortes and Roseilyn Guzman

3. Beyond the Veil: The Black Girl I Could Be   37
   DeLisha Tapscott

4. Refueling: Black Women Leaders Manifesting African Warrior Queenship   53
   Norka Blackman-Richards

PART II: A WOMAN WILL MANIFEST   65
Whitneé Garrett-Walker

5. Life, Love, and Leadership   67
   Rachelle Rogers-Ard

6. The Audacity, Politics, and Pragmatism of Black Women's Leadership   87
   Andrea E. Evans

7	This Too Shall Pass, or Will It? *Roxane L. Gervais and Yetunde Ade-Serrano*	95

PART III: A MORE RADICAL ELSEWHERE — 107
Whitneé Garrett-Walker

8	Keisha vs. Karen: We Ain't Doing This No More! *Renée Heywood and Rhema Heywood*	109
9	Conclusion *Whitneé Garrett-Walker*	115

References	125
Index	141
About the Contributors	148

Introduction

You Are Welcome

Wendi Williams, Whitneé Garrett-Walker, and Nia Spooner

Words like *magic*, *amazing*, and *impressive* are often attached to descriptions of Black women's leadership praxis. It has not always been this way, but of late it seems our wider cultural discourse requires an act of the miraculous to see the leadership of Black women. But why are people impressed? What brings such surprise, really? Our book, this book, *The Majestic Place: The Freedom Possible in Black Women's Leadership*, problematizes the notion, the requirement, of magic and majesty to realize Black women's leadership through the telling of Black women's actual leadership narratives. This book amplifies the stories through the lips of Black women willing to tell that story. The story of ingenuity. The story of struggle. The story of peace. The story of love. The story of community. The story of cultivating a presence and persistence in the darkest of hours and the moments lit up with the light of a thousand inspired hearts. The tales of Black women's leadership do require extraordinary efforts. We do not romanticize the additional effort that we know our male and White counterparts do not have to contend with. We also do not fill our attention with their experience, seduced by the unproductive distraction of what happens in pastures that only appear greener. Rather, we center Black women, Black people whose experiences fall outside the "normative." We decenter the heteronormative, patriarchy-obsessed, essentialist notions of what it means to be Black and rather shift the gaze to *all* the rest of the *us*, over here. We center us and the stories of us told by us who have thrown our hearts and hats in the ring to lead. Welcome to the conversation. Let us now meet our co-editors.

NIA'S WELCOME

The offerings from Drs. Garrett-Walker and Williams, and the essays in this book, not only touch on ideas of refusal within dominant spaces but also made me feel that the experiences I continually pause and reflect on as a Black woman are not unique—they are all too common. While I sit in the comfort of relation and connection to their stories, I also can critically reflect on my own story and consider what has brought me to my work, what I hope for this book, and what the majestic place means to me.

It's taken me many years to learn that I must hold space for myself so I may grow and thrive. From a very young age I struggled to navigate my Chinese and Black identity. Besides being othered from my predominantly White and upper-class classmates, I internalized the unnecessary urge to balance both sides of my heritage, not knowing that it was okay to feel more strongly connected to one identity over the other. Especially living in a world where I am mostly perceived and treated as Black, it took me a while to appreciate the complex ways my Chinese and Bajan heritage intersect and differ in various spaces.

Looking back on the near 10 years I spent teaching elementary and secondary students in the United States, China, and Taiwan, I have experience fighting for and protecting my students from unsupportive school leadership and teachers. Yet I'm still figuring out how to fight for myself. Joining this book project as associate editor has come at a critical transition in my life where I decided to continue my studies in a doctoral program, distancing myself further from practitioner experiences and committing myself deeper into academia. This decision was not easy, mostly because for the longest time I did not view myself as smart and capable enough to pursue a PhD. These thoughts seem ridiculous to me now, as I've grown into myself and realized my own strengths and capabilities. But I am still searching for ways to guide myself out of survival and imposter syndrome mode and further into thriving mode. In carving my path forward in education and leadership, I am learning to be kinder to myself, unlearn traditional ideas of what it means to be a scholar and racialized woman in academia, and stand on the fine line of "playing by the rules" or challenging them.

These offerings, and by extension this book, serve as a grounding and foundational space to learn about the historical and systemic struggles of the Black women leaders before me, as well as a space of hope and joy for our futures, our majestic place. It's also allowed me to consider the ways refusal and liberation have shown up in my life. My father, who passed away when I was young, was a Black man who broke boundaries as an attorney in New York City in the 1980s and 1990s and was constantly challenged in his work. My mother, a first-generation Chinese American woman, broke from tradition and married someone who was both 18 years older than she and outside her race. My older brother, after coming out as gay to our family, learned to reject all White-dominated and heterosexist ideas and embrace his identity. He also taught us that higher education is not the only path one can take to pursue their passions and successes. Each member of my family has been (and will continue to be) oppressed in different ways, and yet they managed to find spaces of joy and liberation. Seeing and understanding their experiences has taught me how I may forge my own passage of refusal.

The complex and rugged path I've taken to embrace my identity has helped me better value myself as a person, an educator, and an academic. I better understand the importance of my presence as a Black and Chinese woman in an academic institution built on exclusivity, colonialism, and whiteness. For me, my leadership journey will involve creativity, collaboration, and kinship—simple yet powerful ideas that have been embedded into the work of Black women educators and leaders for many years. For me, my journey is just beginning.

WHITNEÉ'S WELCOME

I entered this life as Whitneé Louise Garrett-Walker; daughter of Danette and James III; granddaughter of Barbara, Reginald, Michael, Virginia, and James II. I am equal parts sunflower, wife, mother, daughter, sister, and friend. As I enter this sacred space of writing as my whole self, I bring with me former and present selves as a public school teacher, school administrator, and faculty member; surviving cancer, loving life, and carving space for myself to write my truth. I enter this space as a Black, Indigenous (enrolled member of Natchitoches Tribe of Louisiana), and queer woman whose former self was in need of this book in my early years of educational leadership. Entering space is so much more than walking or Zooming into it. It is about intention, understanding the impact, and, finally, creating space for Black women interested in leadership to have a torch to light their darkest days, minutes, hours.

My intention as co-editor of this book is to broaden the scope of what we know about Black women's leadership and the liberation that comes from within it. I remember sitting in my leadership classes preparing to become a school administrator, and I never learned how my leadership, like my teaching, would look very different from the White folx I was working beside. I wanted to learn about the experiences of Black women educational leaders and how to best do my job and maintain my spirit because I knew the work would be hard. I never got the chance to read anything about Black women in educational leadership until I was in my first year as an assistant principal, and by then my spirit was already broken. It was the experiences of women such as Cynthia B. Dillard, Sonya Horsford-Douglass, bell hooks, Patricia Hill Collins, Audre Lorde, Lisa Bass, and Judy Alston that cradled me as I searched for answers. It was the activism of Ida B. Wells-Barnett, the legacy of Dorothy Irene Height, the backbreaking work of my grandmothers and the support of my mentors that gave me the courage to study and add to the scant body of research (and scholarship) regarding Black women and the way we liberate ourselves and those around us with our innovation. Yet no one but Black women will ever understand what we sacrifice in order to hold these positions. My hope is that every Black woman who reads this offering sees themselves reflected and therefore capable of healing, rests in their roles as leaders. My hope for the impact of this offering is that Black women feel as if we are *loving on them* in a way that only *We* can. That they feel seen, understood, validated, and worthy. I invite you to read this book with a glass of your favorite beverage and take note of the many times you smile, laugh, and even cry while reading. I want you to know that we've got you, in the best way.

WENDI'S WELCOME

The majestic place was not always conceived as such. The birth of this book project was spawned out of a desire of our publisher, prior to the pandemic or the murders of George Floyd and Breonna Taylor, to have more titles that centered on the experience of Black women. The world's *woke* critique had begun to reach various industries, and there was a hurried search for scholars and writers who'd long found it difficult to find an outlet for their work. We were now being sought out. I was one such scholar—"discovered" at a convention of the American Psychological Association (APA) in 2019 in Chicago. I was presenting alongside one of the many orphaned graduate students, those unsupported by the faculty at their home institutions, whom I allowed to contribute to and join me in my work so that they'd get some of the academic mentoring they'd been denied. Having experienced my own version of academic abandonment, all the while watching others receive more support and encouragement, I have a particular soft spot for students who ask for help. I know all too well what they need and how my "yes" in such a striking moment of vulnerability can be a vital game changer for their persistence. They are typically Black women, though not always, accepted to these programs because of a unique character and color they add to the diversity goals of an institution, only to be left to flounder. They are the proof of an institution doing better without a structural plan for their personal support and success. I was one such student—until I wasn't. Needless to say, I always say yes when asked to mentor.

Introduction

I brought the book project with me to a new position that involved a cross-country move to an institution experiencing severe challenges. I was welcomed to be dean of a school in desperate need of "turnaround" within a college that was failing and, unbeknownst to me, would be facing its own exigency crises months into my tenure. These are the desperate contexts that Black women, even new and unseasoned leaders like myself at the time, are invited to fail in publicly. The issues facing this institution were long-standing, endemic of poor decision-making, fiscal ineptitude, and an unwillingness to make the type of decisions that, while hard, would have allowed them to survive, even thrive. That school did not, but rather invited a young, vibrant, and ambitious young leader to save it from itself. Before its demise, I encountered a young colleague, barely hanging on; a Black woman who I recognized needed support and an opportunity to shine. She'd begun her career there and, almost from the start, was a causality of the institution's instability. As I thought about the direction in which to take this book project, which, because of my academic privilege and access and the urgency for diverse voices, was handed to me without much articulation of its focus, I invited her to craft it with me. I wanted to share this privilege.

Our first conversations focused on attempting to see an expansive vision of Black women's leadership, ironically as we sat within the confines of an institution burdened by a mix of structural challenge and liberal race and gender politics that allowed for "only so much" transformation. She dreamt of a radicalism she'd never professionally experienced, with a newfound savior (me) powerless against forces that had already written the institution's death certificate. And yet we persisted. With foolish optimism, we imagined *a more radical elsewhere* as the place Black women could lead well. In reality, however, we appreciated that the type of leadership practices we sought to highlight were not possible in the context we currently shared. Wilting beneath the personal challenges brought on by a global pandemic, national health system failures, and, finally, a racial reckoning that refused to turn attention away from the truth of America's racism problem, the project slowed and my colleague ultimately lost stamina.

My light was nearly burned out as well. The veritable canary in the institutional coal mine that is higher education, as a Black woman invited to lead, but not really, my light was flickering to near off. My colleague likely needed to lean on me to stay engaged, while all the while I needed her to show up for me—two broken-winged canaries trying to fly. This is often the experience of Black women in leadership. The espoused celebration of #BlackGirlMagic negates our humanity. The requirement and reliance on magic from the labor of Black women permits a collective narcissism that allows folks to pull from Black women and girls the hard work for the whole group they do not offer to do. To be clear, they are capable; they just allow someone else to do it. In her book *Black Macho and the Myth of the Superwoman*, Michele Wallace

(1979) famously recounts the audacity of a man with whom she was in conversation to say the quiet part out loud. They are seated beside each other, becoming aware of some atrocity in the world, and learn that a nearby Black woman with a sense of responsibility is willing to take on the challenge. Without missing a beat, he thanks goodness there is a Black woman present, because now we know that "it," whatever the problem is, will get fixed. Sounds a lot like the gratitude for Black women's leadership of schools, police departments, cities, nursing stations, COVID vaccine development labs, district attorney offices, etc., we hear now in this late-stage pandemic of flailing capitalistic, would-be democracy.

Admittedly, I am guilty of this gratitude too. Though I know the legacy of *making a way out of no way* taught to me within my community by my mother, grandmother, auntie, and othermothers came at a real cost to them, in a time of crisis I know that I can trust them. I was raised in their image and am also a Black woman that people know they can trust to do the hard thing. That's why I am asked to lead. I already know and, at the same time, must also hold fidelity to my personhood, because unfortunately I also already know that no one else is going to do that for me. No one else is going to ask the question of why the strength of my leadership was not called on before we got to the desperate positionality of no longer having a way. Had I, and many other Black women, been invited to lead earlier, we might not be in such dire straits.

For me the majestic place, the freedom possible in my leadership, is the unwavering love and care I hold for myself and others, the acknowledgment and appreciation of our interiority, our personhood and inherent value and beauty, often overlooked by others to get to what we, Black women, can do for you. The heartfulness, aware of the boundaries and limits that make my opportunities possible, and the openness and awareness that though, wherever I am, I will cultivate and be an articulation of a divine goodness, it will be with deep reverence, appreciation, and care for the goodness that I am. It will be held with profound self-regard and knowledge of the specialness that I am. I own it, unapologetically. And because I am willing and unafraid to see me, I *see* you!

I am aware, without vanity, of the gift that I am/We are, the blessing that I am/We are, the gem that I am/We are. It is with this blessing, this gift, this love that I lead and support the leadership of others and allow others to benefit. And in anticipation of the gratitude the world may or may not have the good sense to convey, I say: *You are welcome!*

THE FREEDOM POSSIBLE IN BLACK WOMEN'S LEADERSHIP

More than anything, *The Majestic Place: The Freedom Possible in Black Women's Leadership* is an invitation. It is an invitation to consider the experiences of Black women leaders writing in their own voice from their own experience from a range of settings. Be it the classroom, the birthing space, the boardroom, the healing space, wherever they are, Black women leading are as much working to create possibilities for their own fullness of being as they are trying to make a way for others.

Resting on the metaphor of the life creations possible through Black birthing people, *The Majestic Place* is Black women's leadership wherein she accesses the presence, purpose, and practice of leading while Black and woman, authentically herself and without apology. The sections "Mother's Milk," "A Woman Will Manifest," and "A More Radical Elsewhere" are stages of becoming the fullest expression of Black women's leadership that allow more and more of her true, authentic self to be present in order for her leadership potential to come into being.

In the "Mother's Milk" section, authors share the seminal her/their stories that nurtured early ideas of Black women's leadership. Our authors explore the formative influences that have shaped their leadership development, at times utilizing the role of mother and mothering as metaphor for this process of becoming. Kaiayo Shatteen urges us to envision motherhood as more than metaphor as they explore the leadership required in the role of midwife in their contribution, "I Never Wanted to Be a Midwife: Stories of Birth." The midwifery of birthing is paralleled with AfroLatinx educational leaders laboring in education contexts whose work, as aptly articulated in the title of the chapter by Krista Cortes and Roseilyn Guzman, "Dando LECHE: Conceptualizing Black-centered Leadership as Mothering Through the *Testimonios* of Two AfroLatinx Higher Education Professionals," is a form of mothering. The section continues with DeLisha Tapscott's recounting of her personal narrative in "Beyond the Veil: The Black Girl I Could Be." This section concludes with Norka Blackman-Richard's "Refueling: Black Women Leaders Manifesting African Warrior Queenship," asserting that Black women's leadership is beyond service—is in fact a form of warriorship—further adding to the conversation amplifying articulation of the interiority of Black women's leadership journey.

A vital understanding that we hold with deep regard and respect is that a woman will, indeed, manifest. We know this without a doubt, as our own lives are proof of that manifestation. In this section, "A Woman Will Manifest," we bear witness to the ways in which Black women's leadership manifests. How it happens and why it is occurring as it does, is viewed from within Black women's gaze and analysis of that leadership practice. The power of personal narrative is seen most prominently in this section of the book through the conversations our authors are having among themselves. Rachelle Rogers-Ard's chapter, "Life, Love, and Leadership," opens the section with her narrative through the cycle of excitement, enchantment, and disappointment in her experience in a system-wide education context.

In the next chapter, "The Audacity, Politics, and Pragmatism of Black Women's Leadership," Andrea E. Evans explores how Black women hold dual identities of marginalized people—Blackness and womanhood—which gives them a unique worldview and uniquely positions them as leaders. She argues that it is within their intersectionality that their power lies.

Roxane Gervais and Yetunde Ade-Serrano pose an essential question for us in "This Too Shall Pass, or Will It?" They wonder aloud with one another about the faith in a better time, a next time, or simply a later time. What allows one to stay in the difficulty that is often associated with leadership, particularly at the intersection of race and gender, for women with darker skin hues? Largely faith, and perhaps other ideals bigger than we are, allows us to stay present when it is simply hard.

The final section, "A More Radical Elsewhere," brings us back to where the early idea of this book began, imagining a place that does not yet exist but that we might have the opportunity of accessing beneath the care, clarity, and persistence of Black women's leadership. This section of the book is speculative as we seek to identify the fullest, most liberated expression of Black women's leadership by imagining what is possible of not only their leadership praxis but also of our world if Black women were to move without apology or care of the persistent structural impediments to their freedom. In this section more than others, our contributors explore a range of creative expressions in the forms of poetry, prose, and song as devices to access the "inner space." As artist Jamila Woods (2016) describes in her song "Way Up": "Just cos I'm born here / Don't mean I'm from here."

What Black women leading must know and access is that sometimes our praxis is deemed otherworldly simply because our leadership of institutions and organizations was never imagined. Like Woods, the contributors to this section explore the key understandings and critical meanings of "elsewhere" necessary to actualize life through the portal we all say we want to go through. One of these imagined inner spaces is a conversation crafted by Renée and Rhema Heywood with a fictionalized White woman serving as an educational gatekeeper for this mother-daughter writing duo. Finally is "The Majestic Place," the piece for which this book was aptly renamed following the transition of co-editorship. Whitneé L. Garrett-Walker's submission to the first iteration of the call for manuscripts of this book chronicles the complexity of accessing the promise of liberatory leadership practices in toxic contexts, our American public school system.

You are invited to join us in this conversation with Black women who lead and, at least in this volume, give a bit more of themselves. Their vulnerability is a gift—not an entitlement but an offering so that we might understand more fully the experience of the leadership journeys they have taken and the moves they continue to make. Making access to this interiority available to others is always a threat for Black women and girls because of how it can be used, misused, and appropriated and then taken for granted. We invite you to look, to take in, to digest, and respect without mishandling. *You are welcome!*

Part I

MOTHER'S MILK
Whitneé Garrett-Walker

Sustenance. Closeness. Nourishment. These are all words that come to mind when thinking of mother's milk. This milk is sweet, packed with antibodies to protect young ones from illnesses and, most importantly, continues to build a sacred bond. An often-misunderstood fact is that similar to birth, the creation of mother's milk requires intense labor. This is labor of the mind to remind your body that it has all it needs to create sustenance. Labor of the spirit to continue the journey even when it gets rough. Labor of the heart when creation of milk isn't possible. Some Black women and birthing people have a very fraught relationship with birth and motherhood/parenthood due to the intergenerational trauma of enslavement and the various ways that we were never able to mother (or be mothered). Yet we found a way to stay alive—and to keep our babies alive. This resistance is important to encapsulate in the metaphor of mother's milk because we carry the sustenance to heal ourselves. This section is first because Black women need to (re)member how to access the well of abundance to replenish ourselves when we are weary. When we were infants, our mothers did this for us. Now that we are mothers, grandmothers, and aunts, we must do this for ourselves. The authors in this section prepared offerings to remind us about what's in the well. It's up to us to tap in and access it.

Chapter 1

I Never Wanted to Be a Midwife

Stories of Birth

Kaiayo Z. Shatteen

I am Kaiayo Zitkála Shatteen; Mother of Jordan Kalani and Sadiq Igwe, Daughter of Beverly and Roy, Granddaughter of Dorthy and Elmon, Great Granddaughter of Bertha and Daniel, Great Great Granddaughter of Ida and Dennis, Great Great Great Granddaughter of Easter and Giles. I never wanted to be a midwife. I had never heard of a doula. Here I am today, a Black Indigenous nonbinary queer femme apprentice midwife. My story begins with the first birth I witnessed.

When I was 12 years old, I witnessed my first birth. My Auntie Winnie was birthing my cousin Martin. I remember begging my mom to let me miss school so that I could come to the hospital. I don't recall too many of the details, yet the important ones stand out. I saw everything. The joy, the pain, the doubt, the triumph. My Auntie Winnie was so strong, I couldn't believe that is what people went through to give birth. At 12 years old, I knew nothing about birthing babies, but after that experience, I fell in love with caring for new mothers and their newborns.

My story continues with birthing my own children. When I was 20 years old, I birthed my son at a hospital in Mountain View, California, and experienced birth trauma. I had just moved out of my mother's apartment, gotten married, and here I was, about to have a baby. My pregnancy was high risk due to atrial fibrillation and cardiomyopathy, which made my labor, birth, and postpartum period risky as well.

On a Saturday night I went to the bathroom and realized that my amniotic waters had opened (I don't say "my water broke" anymore because that gives a negative connotation). I told my partner at the time, and we basically just waited until I started having contractions. I labored through the night on my own while my partner slept, and in the morning around 7:00 a.m., I was ready to go to the hospital. I called my mom and she met us at Labor and Delivery.

I was dilated 4 centimeters upon arrival, and they admitted me. At some point that morning, my labor slowed down and I was told I needed Pitocin to regulate my contractions and keep labor moving. I didn't know what Pitocin was and I don't remember being told; I said OK.

The pain. My God, the pain. My contractions intensified and I felt like I was losing it. I was struggling to breathe, my body felt like it was on fire, and I wanted pain medication. I wanted an epidural and my then-partner said no. My mom begged him because she saw how much pain I was in. He still said no. Looking back, I realize that was the moment when I left my body. I ended up getting Demerol, a narcotic, in my IV, and that helped me regain my breath between contractions yet did nothing for the actual pain of the contractions.

A nurse was really kind and gentle with me. She coached my breathing, held my hand, and told me everything was going to be okay. She helped bring me back into my body to continue laboring to bring my baby earthside. Because of her, I thought I wanted to become a labor and delivery nurse. At some point the doctor, who was White, wanted to check how dilated I was and told me he was going to do a vaginal exam. He shoved his hand through my vulva and up into my vaginal canal. It felt like someone was ripping out my insides, my soul. I immediately shrieked and jumped back away from him. "Do you want me to help you have this baby or not?" he asked. I don't remember my answer because I was gone. The moment I shrieked was the moment I left my body again and didn't come back to it for several hours.

I pushed my son out, and they put him on my chest. My heart was beating so fast, I couldn't catch my breath. All the alarms were ringing, and people were rushing around the room. They took my son from me and began to give me medication to bring my heart rate down. Due to my atrial fibrillation and cardiomyopathy, I was in danger of a heart attack or, worse, heart failure. I could see everyone rushing, worried, scared. It felt like my heart was going to explode out of my chest. I could hear my mom praying and see my then-partner holding our son, frightened. Eventually they stabilized me and then immediately transferred me to the intensive care unit (ICU) without my baby. I needed to be monitored closely, and they weren't able to do that in the postpartum ward. I was monitored by a cardiologist and on medication to keep my heart rate at a normal place.

Being away from my son meant that I didn't get to bodyfeed (breastfeed) him. The nurses were the first ones to feed him, and they fed him with a bottle. I hadn't processed everything that had happened. All I know is that I was thankful to be alive. When I had been stable for several hours, they brought my son to visit me, but I couldn't bodyfeed him due to the medication I was on. It was hours after his birth, and I felt disconnected. Like the time that was taken from us was a million years. He was tiny, cute, and did nothing but sleep. I held him as long as I could before they took him back to the nursery.

I stayed in the ICU for 24 hours. When they were comfortable with my heart rate, they allowed me to go back to the postpartum ward, where I was able to have him in the room with me. I snuggled him, making up for lost time and bodyfed him as much as I could. The next day we went home, and my mother came and spent the night.

That first week was one of the hardest weeks of my life. One night I was alone; my then-partner was out partying with his friends and my mom had gone home. I was trying to latch my baby to my body and I couldn't get it right. He was screaming; I was crying. I recalled the hospital sending us home with bottles of formula. I picked one up and put it in his mouth. He ate while I cried, and then we both went to sleep. That was the end of bodyfeeding for me.

The next couple of weeks were a blur. My then-partner didn't want me to leave the house for 40 days, so I didn't. That meant that most of the time I was home alone with a newborn baby. All I did was feed the baby and cry. I'd lie there, staring at him while he slept, wondering what life would be like if I hadn't had a baby. I would watch him cry and would not move into action to support his needs. I had hit a low that was beyond baby blues. I had postpartum depression. I didn't know it, but my mom did.

One day she came over and told my then-partner that she was taking me and the baby to see my godmother, my Aunt Titi, God rest her soul. That I needed fresh air and help with the baby. He didn't want me to leave, but my mom didn't care. She packed me and the baby up into the car, and we drove out to Antioch. My mom and godmother were my lifesavers. They fed me, let me shower, and allowed me to sleep as long as I needed to. I felt like a new person. Over time, my postpartum depression lifted and I was able to enjoy motherhood.

I was married, 21 years old with a 6-month-old baby, and pregnant again. On a Friday I had my 39-week appointment with my OB-GYN. I told him that I thought my baby was going to come that weekend. He did a vaginal exam and said I wasn't dilated and still had more time. I knew my body and trusted it. After the appointment I called my mom and asked her to spend the night with me and my son in case I went into labor. I didn't want to be alone, as my then-partner was out living his life.

Sure enough, contractions started around 1:00 a.m. I was able to rest through them, breathe through them, and manage the discomfort. Around 8:00 a.m. the contractions slowed down and my mom suggested we take a walk to Walgreens. There I was, waddling down the street, stopping every so often to breathe through a contraction. Once inside, I paused to breathe through a contraction. A woman came up to me and asked if I was in labor.

I told her yes and she wanted to call EMS. I told her that wasn't necessary and that I was fine. She was amazed that I was out walking while in labor. Eventually we made it back home and I took a nap.

A little after 12:00 p.m. I jumped up from my nap and said, "It's time to go!" We got to the hospital around 1:00 p.m. and upon admittance, I was dilated 7 centimeters. A nurse offered me an epidural, and I chose not to get it. Thankfully, a different doctor attended my daughter's birth and it went seamlessly. She was born at 4:34 p.m. and it was beautiful. Gratefully, throughout my pregnancy my atrial fibrillation and cardiomyopathy remained stable and didn't cause any challenges during the postpartum period.

BECOMING A DOULA

My story continues with the second birth I witnessed. My childhood best friend was in labor, and she invited me and another friend to witness her deep transformation. Her husband was having his own experience and struggling to support her. I stepped in and instinctively offered support and care in the ways I thought she needed. I comforted and affirmed her with my words, massaged her back, and held space for all of her emotions.

That friend was birthing at the same hospital where she worked as a labor and delivery nurse. One of her colleagues told me I should be a doula. I had no idea what a doula was.

"You don't want to be a doula. Women are crazy in labor," my friend said. I trusted that advice and didn't think much of it. Besides, I was working 9 to 5 and was not in a place to change careers.

That was in 2014. Sometime between then and 2016, I subscribed to a blog called *Midwives of Color*. I didn't know why I signed up, but I did. There was a posting about a scholarship for BIPOC and LGBTIQA2S+ to attend a doula training. I applied and got in.

Summer of 2016, I resigned from an organization that I had given more than 10 years of my life, began working for the county, and took doula training.

After the training I was grateful for the opportunity to learn but had no idea how I would manage being a doula and working 9 to 5. I decided to focus on my new role and secretly wished I could be a full-time birth worker.

Six months later, in January 2017, I had a choice to become a full-time doula or continue working for other people. I chose to become a full-time birth worker. Kindred Soul Doula became a reality. Thankfully, I had an opportunity to volunteer before fully stepping into the business world.

I mentored with a community doula program based in Oakland. The program was designed to train young people between the ages of 18 and 24 years old to be doulas for their peers, pregnant and birthing people also between the ages of 18 and 24. I got to mentor and support four young people as they took doula clients.

All of my previous work and volunteer experience had been with young adults. Getting to combine youth development and birth work was a dream come true. The wonderful thing about being a mentor is that I also got the opportunity to learn more about birth work and develop my own skills.

While I was volunteering with the program, I was also building a doula practice. I knew nothing about running a business, so one of my very best friends, Ana, introduced me to a birth worker they knew in the community. That's when I met Elena Aurora Aquino, who is now a dear sibling of mine. Elena graciously invited me into her home and talked to me about Roots of Labor Birth Collective (RLBC), a collective of Black, Indigenous, People of Color (BIPOC) birth workers that served primarily BIPOC clients. While getting to know the collective, I learned about the perinatal mortality rates among Black birthing people. I was angry that I hadn't learned about how Black birthing people were dying three to four times more frequently than White birthing people in the first doula training I had taken in 2016. I decided to take another doula training with Elena and RLBC. The knowledge I gained from that training was invaluable.

Here are a couple of journal entries from that training.

Saturday, May 21, 2017, 6:35 a.m.
Today is day 1 of Elena's training. She is the powerful birth worker that has taken me under her wing and allowed me to learn from her wisdom. This week has been tremendous in terms of my doula self growing into an amazing being. I'm stepping into my power, still remaining humble and loving every part of it.

Sunday, May 22, 2017, 6:54 a.m.
Day 2 of the training is this morning. Yesterday was a magical day for me. Realizing what I bring to the table comes to light in different ways, different interactions with folks. Luz is this powerful, radical midwife that I follow on Facebook and Instagram. We gave each other the biggest hug and were happy to finally meet in person. There was a moment during training that I asked a specific question and Luz looked at me and said, "You are thinking and asking questions like a midwife." I had no idea how to digest that other than to know that Spirit was speaking through her to me.

Later that afternoon I was talking to people about potentially wanting to become a midwife and that I was hesitant. All of a sudden, a toddler that was playing with a birth ball bounced so high off of it and flew into the air and landed right into my arms. Everyone laughed and said if that wasn't a sign from the Universe, they didn't know what would be.

On Sunday, May 28, 2017, I wrote a journal entry titled "My Intentions as a Birthworker":

> To heal others through my gentle and kind touch. To be a witness to a parent emerging as their child chooses them. To see life in all forms. In all ways. To be open, honest, and true to myself and my community. To continue learning passionately about how to overcome the systems that oppress our bodies. To show love and courage to birthing people when they think they cannot do it anymore. To help support and guide their journey as they transform into being a parent. To help birthing people find their voice and speak loudly for what they need and deserve. To share knowledge with other birth workers and support their journey. To be of love, of kindness, of joy, of patience, of hope, of determination, of peace.

If I were to write my intentions today, they would definitely be different because of all the learning I have had.

Things changed in the summer of 2017. The program director resigned and the executive director and founder asked me if I wanted the position. I gladly accepted!

As the program director, I would often attend meetings with providers to share information about the program and how their clients could benefit from it. One of the meetings was at Highland Hospital with their midwifery staff. There were about 12 midwives at the meeting and all of them were White. I sat there wondering how all these White midwives could possibly serve BIPOC women while they birthed their legacies. When the founder of the doula program and I left the meeting, I asked her if any Black midwives worked there. She said a few. It was at that moment I thought, *Maybe I should become a midwife*. Yet I had no clue what that would entail.

ANSWERING THE CALL

Our ancestors from Africa carried our birthing traditions and skills when they were enslaved and forced onto Turtle Island. They were the grand midwives. Colonization took midwifery out of the grand midwives' hearts and hands, and in its place, obstetrics and gynecology were established. White men violating the bodies of Black birthing people. A disgrace. Though this country had hundreds of years without the Black midwife at the forefront of a birthing person's journey, there was a new generation that remembered the ways of our ancestors. That carried their legacy.

What can I do? Become a midwife, an ancestor? Me?! Spiritually support a birthing person, provide medical care, and usher a being from the Spirit

Realm?! I was not ready and did everything I could to deny the calling. Finally, with deep meditation and prayer, I answered.

I answered the ancestral call to become a home birth midwife. I was scared as hell, and I did it anyway. In April 2018 I started midwifery school and my life changed. It honestly felt like I had been a midwife all my life. It all came so naturally to me. And it wasn't easy.

May 25, 2018
Midwifery school has been challenging. I need/want to get better at scheduling in study time and find a midwife to apprentice under. That's really nerve-racking for me because it means stepping out of my comfort zone, and that isn't always easy. Like what if they all say no? That's really what I'm afraid of. Why do I think so negatively about myself and my ability to function in this life? What's it going to take, Kai? When are you going to fully love yourself and allow yourself to be happy? It's almost as if I know I can be successful, but I'm just not fully believing in my capabilities.

By August of that year I was working with two licensed midwives as my preceptors, Gingi Allen and Kristen Graser. I was attending prenatal visits, births, and postpartum visits—all while being a doula, mother, and wife. My anxiety was at an all-time high, and I was struggling to juggle all my responsibilities. To numb myself from everything, I started to drink heavily when I wasn't on call.

I was a functional depressed person who drank too much when I wasn't on call for births. That alone made me feel bad about who I was and who I said I wanted to be. I wanted to be a community midwife that people could be proud of. I wanted to be a role model, an example of what it can look like to find your calling.

LOSING AUNTIE WINNIE

That first year ended and a second one began. I continued the day-to-day living of two lives: the doula, midwifery student and the unhappy, alcoholic wife. I know I needed a change; I just didn't know what.

In June 2019 everything shifted. Remember my Auntie Winnie and how I attended her birthing when I was 12? On Thursday, June 6, I was on the phone with her making plans for my daughter's high school graduation the next day. She was going to drive to my house and then ride with me to the graduation. We said "I love you" like we always did and hung up the phone. I didn't know that would be the last time I would speak with her.

The next morning, I had a missed call from her boyfriend and a message saying she was in the hospital. I immediately called my mom to see if she knew, and she was just getting off the phone with Auntie's boyfriend. My mom told me I needed to get to the hospital and see what was going on.

I drove to Fairfield and was by Auntie's side. The story about how she ended up in the hospital still doesn't make sense to me, and I'll continue. She wasn't conscious and machines were helping her breathe. There was little hope that she would wake up, but I prayed anyway.

For several hours I sat by her side, holding her hand and talking to her while she lay in the ICU until I needed to leave for graduation. Whenever we talked to her or kissed her, her heart rate would increase. We saw that as a sign she knew we were there and could make it back. I left that afternoon believing she would wake up and come back to us.

I returned the next day and did the same thing. Sitting by her side, I cried, I prayed, I talked and laughed. I asked her if I would be okay without her and her spirit told me yes. When I came out, she was the only family member that supported me and loved me all the same. I was afraid to be without her. I began remembering all the times she had come over for brunch or dinner. Remembering the time I taught her about the magic of placentas. She always told me that I was becoming a midwife because I attended her birthing. And there I was, attending her transition.

On Sunday, June 9, 2019, she was officially declared brain-dead. My cousin made the tough decision to donate her organs that were viable and remove her from life support. She was at peace; she wasn't suffering anymore. I know there were substances in her system when she passed, and that made me question my drinking to run away from healing.

I meditated and prayed a lot in June. I asked the Creator and my ancestors for guidance on my midwifery journey. I asked them to help heal my broken heart, help me be a better person and a better mother. I asked a lot of them, and they had one question for me: "Are you willing to make the necessary changes in your life?" The day before my Auntie Winnie's memorial service, June 23, 2019, would be the last time I drank alcohol.

BECOMING AN ASSISTANT MIDWIFE

By the time 2020 rolled around, I was embracing sobriety, had divorced my wife, begun tending to my inner child through therapy, and moved into a beautiful cottage in Oakland. My doula business was thriving, I was making my way through my assist phase in school, and my soul felt lighter. I was truly living, and my Auntie Winnie was with me every day.

I never wanted to be a midwife. I had never heard of a doula. Here I am today, a Black Indigenous nonbinary queer femme apprentice midwife. My story continues with the first Black baby girl assigned at birth I received with my heart and hands.

Tuesday, September 15, 2020, I was teaching Childbirth Education over Zoom with the Alameda County Public Health Department. I got a text from one of my preceptors, Gingi Allen, who told me we had a client in labor. I responded, "OK, keep me posted." About 5 minutes later Gingi called me back and told me the client felt like pushing. I needed to drop everything I was doing and get to the client. Before she hung up she told me I would get there first.

I knew exactly what that meant. I would be there to receive the baby without her. I told the participants of the class that I needed to go to the birth and immediately left my cottage. I jumped in the car and headed to the client. "Creator, please carry me safely to the client." "Ancestors, please bless this birth," I prayed out loud as I drove fast yet safe.

I parked, got on and off the elevator, and ran to the client's door. The sitter let me in. I asked if the baby was here yet and she said no. I entered the bedroom, saw the birthing person on her hands and knees, and the partner standing next to her. I went into the bathroom and washed my hands.

"I need to push!"

"OK, breathe and push slowly." Out comes the baby's head and body all in one push. I grabbed the slippery little boo and made sure they were breathing. I immediately passed the baby through the birthing person's legs and into their arms. Tears flowed from all of us, and I said a prayer of thanks. The other midwives arrived, and the rest was a blur. That was the second baby I had ever received as an apprentice.

Several births later and a new year had begun. I had been working so hard as a doula and apprentice that I had forgotten to care for myself. I started to have health challenges and needed to take time off. I spent most of 2021 on leave, and in October I had major surgery.

While I was healing, I questioned whether I was supposed to return to birth work; whether I was supposed to be a midwife. Imposter syndrome was in the back of my mind something fierce. It was as if I had an angel on one shoulder encouraging me to return and a devil on the other making me doubt myself. I figured I would wait for a sign from the Universe.

I decided to ease my way back into midwifery by taking a doula client. My chosen family, Ana and Nee, were having a baby and asked me to be present at their birth. I told them it all depended on how I was feeling and that I would try my hardest to make it. As the guess date for the birth got closer, I felt ready to be present.

On Friday, December 17, 2021, Ana called to tell me she was having some contractions. She said they were slightly painful but still manageable. We were both super excited and decided we would stay in touch over the weekend; she would let me know if anything changed.

The next day she texted me that the contractions "kinda went away" and that she was a bit disappointed. I listened to her and validated all her feelings, and we both went about our days.

On Sunday Ana called to tell me that the contractions had returned and were stronger than before. I asked if she was ready for me to support her and she said yes! I was out running errands, so I told her to take a bath to try and ease the discomfort.

I was still out running errands when I got a call from their midwife. She told me that things seemed to be progressing and that she was going to head over there in an hour or so. I told her I was heading over soon after my errands, and she said that was fine. Not even 5 minutes go by, and the midwife calls back and asks me to head over there right away. She wanted to get an assessment of how things were going and was getting ready to head over as well.

I didn't know what I was going to walk into; all I knew was that Ana was in labor, it was progressing, and they needed support. I forgot about my last errand and headed to their home. They lived in Vallejo, so I knew it would take me some time to get there. I said my usual prayers, "Creator, please carry me safely to the client. Ancestors, please bless this birth," as I drove fast yet safe.

On the way to their home, the midwife called again to tell me the baby was coming and that I would be the first one to get there. She wouldn't make it in time and wanted me to call her as soon as I got there. While I was driving, Nee, Ana's spouse, was texting on our group thread that Ana was bleeding and they were starting to get worried. I used the talk-to-text feature on my phone to tell them I would be there soon. Nee asked my estimated time of arrival; it was 7 minutes.

Those 7 minutes felt like a lifetime. I parked and ran into the house. Ana was on her hands and knees, tears streaming down her face, drenched in sweat; Nee was next to her, singing "Darling" by Beautiful Chorus. I got close to Ana and rubbed her back. She had a surge, and it sounded like a grunt. As an apprentice, I knew that meant the baby would be born soon. I called the midwife and had her on speaker phone like she requested. She told me where the gloves were, and Ana said, "I'm scared." "It's OK, I've done this before," I said as I slipped on a glove. I looked between Ana's legs and could see the baby's head. "I see a little bit of the head!" I called out to the midwife.

Ana had a strong surge, let out a deep groan, and the baby's head emerged. "Head!" I yelled, and before the midwife could respond I yelled, "Body!" The baby came out with their umbilical cord wrapped around their body, and I somersaulted them to get them untangled. I held the little boo and made sure they were breathing. They started crying, and I felt relieved. Thank the Creator! Thank you, ancestors!

"Ana, here's your baby." Ana didn't respond, and Nee said, "Here, I'll take the baby." I passed the baby to Nee through Ana's legs and then handed the baby to Ana. They looked into each other's eyes and then back down at the baby and started crying. I lay Ana down, and we all continued to cry. The rest is a blur.

Remember how I said I was waiting for a sign from the Universe to see if I was supposed to return to birth work and midwifery? Well, receiving my soulmate, Nazreen Ayo Dioni James Gomes, was the only sign I needed. Since December 2021 I have continued to attend births as a doula and an apprentice midwife.

I am currently in my primary phase, the last part of school! I continue to work with Gingi Allen and am now working with Anjali Sardeshmukh, Ana's midwife. It's challenging, and there are times I want to give up. When I have those moments, I remember the legacy of the grand midwives.

Mama Claudia was 71 years old when she became an ancestor in 2020. Mama Afua was 62 years old when she became an ancestor in 2021. Through social media, I was blessed to interact with them about the joys and pains of Black midwifery. They spent their lives midwifing families and mentoring young Black midwives. I have a picture of Mama Claudia and Mama Afua on my altar, and I honor them every day. When I want to give up on midwifery school, they are there to remind me of my strength, that the strength of the grand midwives is in my heart and hands. Though I never met either one of them, they are me and I am them.

I never wanted to be a midwife. I had never heard of a doula. Here I am today, a Black Indigenous nonbinary queer femme apprentice midwife. My story continues. My only hope is that I can make my ancestors proud.

Chapter 2

Dando LECHE

Conceptualizing Black-Centered Leadership as Mothering Through the Testimonios of Two AfroLatinx Higher Education Professionals

Krista L. Cortes and Roseilyn Guzman

"*Mi leche es amor*"/"My milk is love" is a song by Karla Kanora that describes mother-child bonding through the act of breastfeeding: "I imagine what your voice sounds like/I know that you envision me holding you tight and wrapping my arms around you." In giving of their milk, the mother is not thinking of her/their relief from the pain of engorgement, for example, but rather of the benefits the child experiences from this nourishment—a special and almost sublime energetic exchange. Our literal *leche* offers up essential nutrients and antibodies, while the act of holding one's baby skin-to-skin for a sustained period also transmits emotional and cognitive benefits to the beloved other. This transference of milk becomes liminal gesture, process, and action; and *leche*, as essence, as bond, becomes a spiritual offering and connection-mechanism which draws from the mother's person while flowing a supporting embrace toward the other. An offering of love so that the beloved may thrive. "*Mi leche es amor.*"

For Black women/folks, the way we lead in higher education looks a lot like mothering. When we consider mothering beyond the biological and imagine it instead as a social practice (Dewi Oka, 2016), we move through a world where the "production of knowledge begins in the bodies of our mothers, and grandmothers, in the acknowledgment of critical practices of women of color before us" and shifts into the lived realities we seek to create through our actions (Cruz, 2001, as cited in Duran, 2019, p. 658). As AfroLatinx leaders, our work often requires us to be storytellers, keepers of knowledge, and innovators of Black futures. As mothers/mother figures, we are called to birth and rear the next generation and teach important lessons about how to live and thrive in a white supremacist, settler-colonial, capitalist heteropatriarchal society. Through our bodies (and our essence/presence), we give life—feeding the survival and joy of Black people. As mothers and leaders, we devote ourselves to building relationships that strengthen our communities and uplift our people. Yet, within the systems and structures we lead where we engage in multifaceted care, we often find ourselves "overused, misunderstood, and unappreciated" (Anaya, 2011, p. 22), and still we continue to give of ourselves—our *leche*/milk—mothering (people, communities, institutions, movements) as a means to "reimagine, reconstruct, and thrive in utopias of hope" (Duran, 2019, p. 151).

In this chapter we explore leadership as a form of mothering done from AfroLatinx bodies, specifically as it relates to the idea of milk as sustenance. We situate our writing within the literature on AfroLatinx feminisms, mothering, and leadership to show the ways our identities as AfroLatinx leaders and mothers are co-constituted and entwined in how they impact our work in higher educational spaces. Our findings come from a qualitative study that uses the methodological tool of *testimonios* to center personal herstories and bodymindspirit as sites from which we theorize (Lara, 2005). By "theorizing our own realities," we offer a window into our varied experiences of/with AfroLatinidad—how, through our leadership roles, we have embraced our Blackness and Latinidad and mothered others in our communities to do so as well (Peréz Huber, 2009, p. 643). From this storytelling we offer up our "homemade theory" (Duran, 2019, p. 147) of *dando LECHE* (giving milk) to describe the ways we feed our communities toward liberation. *LECHE* becomes a heuristic for understanding AfroLatinx leadership as mothering: **L**eading with love; **E**mpowering communities, each other, and ourselves; **C**ompass(ionate) guidance, **H**onoring our her/their stories; **E**xpansive and transformative praxis.

THEORETICAL GROUNDING

Our overlapping and intersecting identities shape the context for our leadership; being Black, being women/gender diverse, being a particular ethnicity and age are multiplicities of being which influence the ways our leadership is embodied and enacted (Alexander, 2010; Bass, 2012; Byrne-Jiménez & García, 2021; Garcia, 2018; Grant, 2012; Horsford, 2012; Horsford & Tillman, 2012). Understanding the context from which our leadership derives is an important step toward "fleshing out" theories of leadership in order to reflect "the physical realities of our lives—our skin color, the land or concrete we grew up on, our sexual longings—all fuse[d] to create a politic born out of necessity" (Moraga, 1981, p. 23). We bring together various strands of literature to ground us in an understanding of AfroLatinidades and AfroLatinx feminisms as they relate to conceptions of mothering and leadership.

AFROLATINX FEMINISMS

For AfroLatinx people who move through the world as Black, we often experience possibilities of erasure because we are neither embraced as Black nor seen/regarded as Latine (Hoy, 2010; Jorge, 2010; Lara, 2012; Rivera-Rideau, 2017). Institutions like schools and families figure prominently in the policing of borders between Blackness and Latinidad, with overwhelming effect on Black Latina bodies (Cortes, 2019; Jorge, 2010). This erasure is so prevalent, Lara (2012) writes, "[AfroLatinx people] don't even appear as a sector in statistical data, because the data is not segregated by ethnic composition [creating an] assumption of the inexistence of our race" (p. 303). We are called to reposition AfroLatinx people and AfroLatinidades as a "domain of difference" and "oppositional form of political identity" in order to necessarily challenge colonial logics that have sought to diminish the existence and importance of AfroLatinx communities' ways of knowing and being (Laó-Montes, 2005, p. 118). We are valid in our many intersections and, as such, new conceptions of AfroLatinidades require a move away from nationalistic conflations of ethnicity and race as we acknowledge "blackness as a site of rupture" (Lopez Oro, 2020, para. 14). This demands us to dig deeper and move past Blackness as a monolith to get at the intricacies inherent in the Black diaspora; we must interrogate the "empty spaces . . . where as AfroLatina women, we cannot locate ourselves" (Zamora, 2017, p. 7).

AfroLatinx feminisms enter this rupture to contend with the "overlapping histories of racialization, colonialism, and dispossession that are endemic to diasporic experiences" while fully recognizing "Afro- Latina/o/x lived experiences [in order to] . . . be faithful witnesses to Afro-Latinas who find themselves at the crossroads of covert and overt racism and indifference" (Figueroa, 2020, p. 2). By adopting transnational AfroLatinx feminist perspectives, we prioritize the daily practices of women of African and Latin American heritage, emphasizing the knowledge and power they wield to assert influences in the spaces they inhabit (Plácido, 2017). An AfroLatinx feminist approach allows us to push against a Black/Latinx either/or dichotomy in order to see the fluidity between these positionalities and the complexity in how gender, Blackness, and Latinidad intersect in lived experiences of leadership and mothering as a means to "offer practical guidelines to address the leadership demands of changing organizations in contemporary society" (Ospina & Foldy, 2009, p. 876; Plácido, 2017; Zamora, 2017). It is only through telling our myriad stories of being/becoming AfroLatinx feminists that we are able "to construct as varied a definition of our existence as possible, in as many ways as possible [so we can] be free in the world" (Lara, 2012, p. 44).

MOTHERING

Black feminist views of mothering center the lived experiences of gender, race, and class as they intersect and influence the political act of designing for the learning of Blackness (Crenshaw, 1991; Gumbs, 2016; hooks, 2014). Through our intersecting identities, AfroLatinx women have found ways to center and support the collective learning and unlearning of wide-ranging understandings of Blackness (Cortes, 2020). AfroLatinx women learn to mother children, adults, and themselves toward the survival of Black people as "part of the larger human struggle for greater peace, beauty, freedom and justice" (Abdullah, 2012, p. 57; Caballero et al., 2019; Gumbs, 2016). Mothering requires AfroLatinx women to occupy multiple roles, simultaneously acting as cultural workers, ancestral knowledge-bearers, standard setters, and the orchestrators of worldviews for the Black community writ large (Cortes, 2020; Radford-Hill, 1986; Segura & Facio, 2008).

AfroLatinx people are not immune to societal norms that impose historic and culturally gendered ways of being. The expectation and need to "take care of" others often shapes Latina leadership (Byrne-Jiménez & García, 2021). Latina scholars have described higher education's reliance on "gendered, classist and racialized notions of mothering" (García-Louis & Reyes-Barriéntez, 2022, p. 1) and the ways this impacts what kinds of productivity and participation are valued in academic spaces to the detriment of those who mother (Caballero et al., 2019; Matias, 2011). We attempt to trouble the colonial gender system (Lugones, 2010) and heteronormative understandings of how Latinx people mother and lead by situating our understandings of leadership as mothering within the idea of *AfroBoriqua mothering*, which emphasizes mothering among Black diasporic kinfolk as proleptic and political as well as an action that exceeds normative constructions of gender toward revolution and the creation of socially just worlds (Cortes, 2020). We pair this with the conception of *MALA MADRE*, which seeks to transform spaces like educational institutions "into reflections of our historical truths and cultivating futures rooted in social justice and collective action for liberation" (Duran, 2019, p. 155). Through a Black-centered leadership approach, AfroLatinx mothers seek to model truth and affirm hope by bringing our "bold, brilliant, unapologetic" selves into our work with the goal of transforming the spaces and institutions we lead toward "love, progress, and freedom" (Duran, 2019, p. 156).

LEADERSHIP

Building from Indigenous understandings of leadership, we conceptualize leading as vision setting rather than management. Kenny (2012) suggests that our first encounter with leadership comes from our relationship to the Earth, known in Andean Indigenous communities as *Pachamama*: "the feminine creative power to sustain life on earth" (Medina & Gonzales, 2019, p. 7). Our being and existence is based on our relationality to Earth as our first mother, and this forms the basis of how we understand interconnectedness and reciprocity (Medina & Gonzales, 2019), core pieces of how we conceptualize impactful and intentional leadership. Lifting up and centering the knowledge that comes from being in communion with land and the spaces we occupy is essential to creating spaces that are reflective of our collective experiences (Matias & Liou, 2015; Urrieta, 2007) and that foster consequential leadership grounded in reciprocity (Castagno, 2021).

We also come to understand leadership through the "guidance of the processes expressed in our home place," which we see as akin to the various ways we cultivate and experience community in our lives (Kenny, 2012, p. 3). One way this manifests is through instantiations of *compradazgo* within higher education settings. *Compadrazgo* has strong connections to AfroLatinx religious and spiritual traditions where *comadres* (co-mothers) and *compadres* (co-fathers) offer guidance to their *ahijado* (godchild) in their spiritual upbringing (Ebaugh & Curry, 2000; Wirtz, 2007). Higher education settings often necessitate women of color to replicate these kinds of support systems at work in order to survive (Anaya, 2011). Garcia-Louis and Reyes-Barriéntez (2022) describe the importance of academic *comadres* in higher education for the support and community they provide in the workplace as well as the important roles they play in our personal/familial lives. These types of relationships allow us to "imagine liberation in our homes, at work, and in our communities through the enactment of modes of resistance that delegitimize and destabilize extant systems of oppression" (Garcia-Louis & Reyes-Barriéntez, 2022, p. 11).

All of these theoretical insights help us to imagine AfroLatinx feminist mothering as leadership that creates space for holistic ways of being that are sustainable, impactful, and focused on dismantling oppressive institutions that repress Black life (Greene Brown, 2020).

Following mothers' lead, higher education needs to allow leadership to embody the scripts of Blackness that are rooted in the collective experiences of Latinx people in the African diaspora (Cortes, 2020; Garcia-Louis & Cortes, 2020; Godreau, 2015). Through a concerted and targeted effort to make space for AfroLatinx-centric discourse and sensibilities, higher education must disrupt normative approaches to leadership by creating multiple centers of knowledge, such as Indigenous and Third-World knowledges, rather than privileging solely one (Dei, 2000, 2017). AfroLatinx mothering itself is a source of knowledge, as it specifically calls attention to the "Black borderlands" of Latinidad through critical transnational feminist praxis that seeks liberation and decolonization in the Latinx and Black communities (Laó-Montes, 2007, p. 316). Bringing an AfroLatinx feminist perspective to higher education leadership gives us a landing space for understanding how AfroLatinidades as a way of being is intimately connected to care. When leaders embrace our full humanity (Darder, 2017; hooks, 1994; Paris & Winn, 2014; Smith et al., 2018), leadership becomes more about collaboration, making connections between and across subjectivities and knowledges and less about asserting authority (York-Barr & Duke, 2004).

TESTIMONIOS AS METHODOLOGY AND METHOD

This work is framed by *testimonio* as both methodology and method. As a methodology, we understand *testimoniando* as a process that "provides modes of analysis that are collaborative and attentive to myriad ways of knowing and learning in our communities" (Delgado Bernal et al., 2012, p. 364). The action of *testimoniando* is an affront to the many oppressions that seek to attack our intersecting identities and take away our power. *Testimoniando* creates opportunities for "healing through the collective identification that emerges when struggles are voiced to those with a shared understanding" (DeNicolo & Gónzalez, 2015, p. 111). As such, the process of sharing a *testimonio* challenges Eurocentric notions of what counts as knowledge and troubles the traditional roles of researcher and research subject to position one's intuition and bodymindspirit as legitimate sources of knowledge to be studied and learned from (Lara, 2005).

As a method, *testimonio* is the product that comes from telling one's truth. While having many definitions, we refer to *testimonio* as "an account told in the first person . . . evolving from events experienced by a narrator who seeks empowerment through voicing [their] experience" (Blackmer Reyes & Curry Rodríguez, 2012, p. 527). This "embodied narrative" is shared with the purpose of bringing about change (Elenes, 2013, p. 137). *Testimonio* is different from other methods, such as oral history or life stories, "in that it calls upon the participant to share a critical reflection of their personal experience within particular sociopolitical realities" (Delgado Bernal et al., 2012, p. 364). We choose this method because we are both researchers and participants seeking to theorize from our own positionalities; as such, our *testimonios* become a space for "delineating the geographies, axes, and *vaivenes* that structure

[our] conceptualization of Black Latinidad as a site for critical engagement" (Garcia Peña, 2022, p. 2).

PROCESS AND POSITIONALITY

As AfroLatinx women we carry stories of both our African and Latinx ancestral backgrounds as they inform the ways in which we embark on our individual paths and choose to navigate spaces. We share our positionality as it deeply impacts our approach to this research. Krista identifies as an Afro-Puerto Rican born and raised in the diaspora. They spent their childhood in New York before moving around the country pursuing various degrees while finding their purpose. Over the many years that Krista lived and was in community with other Afrodiasporic people, their activist spirit was awakened, which has guided them as the mother of two Black boys and as a teacher-scholar mothering a community. Roseilyn identifies as AfroDominican, born and raised in the Dominican Republic until the age of 8. She spent her childhood being raised by her mother and the matriarch of their family, *abuela* (grandmother) Carmen, and surrounded by her *tías* (aunts), from whom she gained her wisdom, courage, and joy—all qualities she centers as a leader. She used their love and teachings to cope with the process of assimilation into what she considered a new world (the United States). In search of unconditional support, she found belonging and sisterhood with Afrodiasporic women leaders.

We are not only co-authors but also co-workers, serving as director and associate director, respectively, of the Center for Hispanic Excellence: La Casa Latina at the University of Pennsylvania. In its 23 years of existence, we are the first Afrodescendants to hold leadership positions at the center. As AfroLatinas working together in this space, we are constantly taking inventory of our partnerships, impact, and individual journeys. Working together has given us the opportunities to merge our different worlds, experiences, and perspectives as we simultaneously embody leaders who mother and teachers who learn.

Taking inventory of our work and relationships has enabled us to reflect on how our past informs, and continues to inform, our current decisions and our collective vision for the future. We mirrored this process in preparing to write this chapter by engaging in a recursive and iterative process of journaling, conversations, and reflections which fed into our *testimonios*. Initially we began with conversations to situate us in the topics of leadership, mothering, and AfroLatinidad. These conversations inspired pages of jottings where we recorded the various ways we understood these topics on their own, then in relation to one another. We oscillated between our conversations and personal journaling to reflect then dive deeper into our individual positionalities and the spiritual and inherited knowledge forms that guide us. After several iterations of journaling and conversation, we developed the following questions to help shape our *testimonios*:

- How do you understand/define *leche*/"mother's milk" and how has it manifested in your work as an AfroLatinx leader?
- How do you live and experience your AfroLatinidad?
- How do you understand leadership?
- How is mothering connected to your leadership?
- Who has inspired you in your construction of a leadership identity?

OUR *TESTIMONIOS*

Our *testimonios* highlight the core essence of how we came into ourselves and also our calling into leadership. They highlight how our intersectional identities guide us to lead from a Black-centered leadership approach: our *leche*—the manifestation of love and care for those we serve and support. This process continues to encourage us to reflect on our challenges, struggles, and progress, all while remembering that there will always be work to be done. In the same ways that *cafecito* (coffee) time and *charlas* (chats) provide AfroLatinx people with space to be in community as we release our burdens in cathartic hopes of healing, we share our *testimonios* as a means toward self-making and reclaiming our agency.

We choose to share our *testimonios* with you in their raw form in order to give you a window into our lived experiences. Having this snapshot of our lives creates an opportunity to learn from our journeys to reach our most authentic selves. It can be difficult to open up and share our stories at times, but in order to create safe and inclusive spaces where we can exist with our multiplicity, we need to own our story in order to appreciate our uniqueness and recognize our worthiness. By doing so, we hope to encourage others to do the same. We ask that you approach our stories with care and compassion; in turn, we hope they offer some illumination of our paths of becoming Black-centered leaders and mothers.

Fierceness and Care: A *Testimonio* About Growing Into an AfroLatinx Leader

"*Mamá, leche.*" It's a phrase I have become accustomed to hearing multiple times a day over the past 6 years. "*Mamá, leche.*" Sometimes it comes to me as a soft whisper from a sleeping child, seeking me out for comfort in the middle of the night. "*Mamá, leche!*" It can also be a cry that crashes down on me from an inconsolable child that can't make sense of where my body ends and theirs begins, in the process of learning about boundaries of body, in the emotional realm of need. My milk has been something I have been so proud of—the gift of sustaining my children through my body's magic. Breastfeeding is a journey I set out on without guidance or examples for how to get started and turn into a sustained practice. I chose to breastfeed because it was something I felt in my soul that I wanted to do for me and my children. "Are you sure you want to do that?" "Shouldn't you cover up?" "Your children *still* nurse?" And somehow I found a way to make it work despite those who questioned me or doubted my choices. My body, my breasts, my children—we reclaimed space for Black mothering, Black life, and Black joy.

After 6 years of breastfeeding two AfroLatinx boys, I now struggle with wanting to take back control of my body. I can't remember what it is like to not be at the beck and call of someone else. Who am I apart from my *leche*, my milk? This is a feeling that comes and goes. "*Mamá, leche?*" A question posed with bashful eyes when he can sense my frustration and is trying to melt my hardened exterior. Holding my youngest as he nurses, being in the moment and succumbing to the connection we have gets me through. Seeing my oldest flourish without the need for my physical milk, but still being nourished in the many other ways I feed his being, I know my body will return to me one day and I will give of myself in other ways. "*Mamá*, I want my *leche*." A reminder that the milk I produce is not mine alone but is a shared, collective thing. I love that my children have seen the milk as theirs, something that is quintessentially made uniquely for them.

This reframing is a helpful reminder about the ways I use my body to uplift and fuel others—spiritually, emotionally, mentally, physically, and beyond. All the ways seen and unseen. I see many parallels across my life experiences; a familiar trend that reappears time and again of how I made a way out of no way, turned a dollar into a dime. As I reflect on my journey into motherhood and my relationship with my/our milk, I see similarities in how I came into other identities I possess and the means I have employed to nourish myself even when it felt like no one or thing cared about my survival.

I never had a mentor who identified as AfroLatinx. The first time I was in a classroom with a Black teacher was in graduate school. Growing up I didn't think much of it. My Blackness wasn't discussed openly. It would be too easy, and quite frankly wrong, to say my family was/is anti-Black. Rather they were non-Black people raising a Black child and had no manual or resource to guide them on that journey. When it comes to pigmentation in the Latinx community writ large, anything is possible—from the palest complexion with blonde hair and blue eyes to the darkest skin you've seen; we aren't any one thing. And our Blackness is not just how we present phenotypically but is also imbued in our cultural practices and ways of being. My mom did not know what to do with my tightly curled hair, but she tried. My cousins always picked me to be Scary Spice, the only Black member of the group, when we were playing pretend (cue the Spice Girls song, *Spice World* the movie, and '90s nostalgia). I always knew I was Puerto Rican, but I never quite articulated myself as Black because I never felt empowered to do so. I was told not to spend time in the sun for fear I would get too dark. I was advised to massage my nose to keep it from getting "too wide." Other than my father, who I did not see much in my early years, there was no one in my immediate family that looked like me; there was no one to help me make sense of the othering I felt and *lived* at home and school, the two spaces in which I primarily existed.

I didn't realize the immense weight of not seeing myself reflected in the world, nor reflected back to me, until I started college. It was then that I began to come into my Blackness, to embrace myself as a Black person in the world. I joined a historically Black sorority, Zeta Phi Beta, where the women accepted me as Black *and* Puerto Rican, giving me the space to be my full self. I am forever indebted to them for this because—for the first time in my life—I was able to surround myself not only with Black folks but also folks from the African diaspora who lived their Blackness in its beautiful multiplicity.

My first stint in graduate school gave me an opportunity to put forth a new, more authentic version of myself. It was at this point in my life that I began to name myself as AfroPuerto Rican. Notice that my Blackness and Puerto Ricanness came together in a way that felt right, which I had never been able to express before. I loved who I was becoming, and I started reading and educating myself about the history of Black people in Latin America and the Caribbean (this was also around the time I learned that while Afro, Celia Cruz was not Puerto Rican but Cuban). In learning about the life of Celia Cruz, I learned how I can use my talents, like being an educator and creative, to bring awareness to issues of social justice. In reading the memoir of Marta Moreno Vega, I learned about the power of our ancestors and the strength of body memory in attuning us to our purpose and setting us on our path. Hearing the stories of Fermina Gómez Pastrana, the mother of Cuban Santería, I became fortified in the ways women can be leaders in a world dominated by men. I found refuge in the poetry of Victoria Sanchez and Mariposa, whose words spoke life into my experience as an AfroLatinx person in this society. In the characters created by Dahlma Llanos-Figueroa and Aya de Leon, I saw myself and the other worlds and ways of being that were possible for AfroLatinx people. These characters and life worlds also taught me a lot about mothering and what community-informed leadership could look like. In the spiritual activism of Destiny Nicole Frasqueri, I have become more emboldened to live a public life led by my spirituality.

At this point in my journey, I became focused on spirituality and religion—what did our ancestors believe and practice? I started to read about the Yoruba people and Lukumi traditions and was fascinated by all I found in the books I couldn't help but devour. This set me on my path (and perhaps I was always on this path) toward initiating into Santería as a priestess of Oyá. This was one of the pivotal moments that shaped my understanding of AfroLatinx feminisms, mothering, and leadership. The orisha/santos—beautiful Black deities—provide countless examples of mothering that defy gender: Blackness as varied and powerful; leadership as fierceness and care. In our religious tradition, initiates are born unto a particular orisha, who becomes their protector and guide in life; in turn, the initiate or child vows to honor that orisha. It is freeing for me to think about how, no matter the gender expression of the orisha (some orisha can present as both female or male or androgynous), our orisha in many ways mothers the child through the life course of their religious practice. Sometimes this mothering looks like *consejos*—a metaphysical embrace, tough love, or stepping in to protect one from harm, to name but a few manifestations. While the orisha seek to guide their children, they allow for agency and self-expression—qualities I seek to exhibit through my own leadership.

As I grew into adulthood, I sought out Black female mentors; I knew there was a lot to be learned from their experiences navigating the academy as scholars and higher education as an institution. But I never could get it right. Not having something for so long, I put too much on the relationships when they unveiled and then placed unrealistic expectations on the both of us. Failing at this was heartbreaking, but I also learned so much about how to be a femtor and leader. Given how few of us actually make it into leadership positions, it is no wonder there is an untenable expectation to serve "our community"; to "show up" for the Black, Brown, AfroLatinx students and be their reflection in an otherwise oblique environment. Yet it is impossible to meet the needs of so many students when those needs are so diverse. *Leche* is as much spiritual as it is nurturing caregiving, but sometimes what is needed goes unuttered, and/or when we are nursing too many bodies, our supply, our bodies, stall—until we replenish again.

My style of leadership is best described as leading by example. Taking into consideration my own safety and the limitations ingrained into academic spaces, I attempt to bring my full self to work. This means being unapologetically AfroLatinx, comfortable mothering in my gender fluidity in the workplace, committed to creating a world for Black and Brown joy, and a forever learner. I try to lead through intuition and love, honoring the knowledges I carry with me from my ancestors and elders. Caring for my community, those who seek me out as a leader in both formal and informal ways, is my utmost priority and what my life experience thus far has taught me is always needed.

Courage and Resilience: A *Testimonio* About Merging Two Worlds to Become an AfroLatinx Leader

At 8 years old, my parents made a decision that would change our lives forever: to emigrate from the Dominican Republic to the United States. This decision was coupled with what felt like two insurmountable goals: to learn English and to succeed academically. As I began to navigate the fears, doubts, and shame associated with being labeled an ESL (English as a second language) student in middle school, I quickly realized that courage and resilience were going to be my tools for survival in this foreign environment. Despite the challenges I faced in the process of assimilating to a new culture and customs, there was one thing that remained the same—my mother's *chocolate con leche*. Her *chocolate con leche* served many purposes in my transition. Indulging in a cup of this dark brown, sugary, milky substance was nourishing for both my body and soul. It was the reminder of the morning routine I had with my *abuela* Carmen before walking to school. Furthermore, it became a taste of nostalgia, a remembrance that although we were a sea apart from our loved ones, we brought a piece of them with us into our new world.

Along with the pot of hot chocolate, there was also a note that my mother wrote every week and left for me on different pieces of paper: "*Acuérdate de tomarte tu chocolate con leche y comparte con tu hermano*" ("Remember to drink your hot chocolate and share with your brother"). My mother's goal was not only to provide a warm drink in the mornings but also to leave a pot for us filled with many valuable lessons. This was her act of love, care, and nourishment. By leaving us a pot of *chocolate con leche*, she exemplified what a mother's sacrifice looks like, as she had to wake up at 3:00 a.m. and be ready to leave for work at 4:30 a.m. daily. In addition, she taught me how we can positively use our past to guide our present, how one's traditions can be introduced and kept alive in new communities, and the importance of sharing with our loved ones. Love—as *leche*—as reminder notes/lessons on the important connections within and around us, as creative motherly presence— has always been a transference of the everyday mixed in with little blessings. As I continued on my journey, this sustenance gave me the strength to survive, thrive, and find joy living in the in-between. A single cup of *chocolate con leche* gave me the encouragement I needed to embrace that I could be *de aqui y de alla* (from here and over there).

Though I wanted to feel confident living in this new normal, I realized that learning English was not going to be the biggest challenge I would face; it was going to be knowing how to identify myself in a Black-and-White America. As my English progressed and I started to develop relationships with my peers, their initial way of connecting with me was by asking, "What are you?" I remember pausing every time. This was my first introduction to the disparities between my racial and ethnic backgrounds and the American obsession with having to check one binary box as laid out by the US census. For many years, my response was the same: "I am a first-generation immigrant, an ESL student, and Dominican." But the looks on my peers' faces always left me wondering whether I was identifying myself correctly. To them, I did not look "Latina enough" because my phenotypic features did not resemble those of the actors they saw in telenovelas; neither did I sound "Black enough" because I had a Caribbean accent.

In search of an acceptable response for myself to myself—and, so, to others—I would often ask my parents after school, "What am I?" To which they responded: *"Tu eres Dominicana, mi hija. No entiendo la pregunta."* ("My daughter, you are Dominican. I don't understand the question.") I often left these conversations feeling hopeless and uncertain because I did not know if I was ever going to know how to identify myself. Even though I did not have what felt like the "right" answer to give my peers, I was learning that I did not want to fall into society's rules of having to choose one identity over the other. These childhood experiences held me in a prism until I accepted that I could exist both in a solely Spanish-speaking household and in outside-world Black(-American) affirming spaces. Although my parents did not have the educational tools and language to name our home a Black-affirming space, they embraced and celebrated our Blackness with their actions. They instilled in me the importance of attending *palo* gatherings, taking *bomba y plena* dance lessons, and openly expressing their appreciation for the beautiful and unique phenotypic differences that exist within our families.

As I grew into accepting these dual realities (which were also one and the same), I immersed myself in both Dominican and Black-American culture, using the cultural teachings and traditions around me to create a world in which I could blend what felt like two orbits into one. All valid parts of who I was, and who I was becoming.

Growing up in the North Philadelphia community, I was surrounded by strong, dedicated, powerful women who maybe did not identify as AfroLatinx but who moved in a way that celebrated their cultural backgrounds with the utmost pride; from their accents to their hairstyles, they embraced all of who they were. In them, I found my mother's *leche* outside of my kitchen at home. Although I did not grow up seeing AfroLatinx leaders around me, I found solace in listening to Celia Cruz, Alicia Keys, Jordin Sparks; watching Tony Dandrade and La Chiky Bombom; and reading Maya Angelou. It did not matter that they did not all identify as Dominican, only that they were role models and leaders in their respective fields. In my educational settings I gravitated to femtors who embodied the personality traits of my mom and aunts. I fostered mentoring relationships early in my middle school years, where I found myself being mothered by a Black(-American) science teacher and a Puerto

Rican front desk receptionist. These women were the representation that I could do anything in life.

My femtors taught me the power of collaboration, showing me that who I was, my aspects of self, could not exist without what others had made to be counter. I embodied *de aqui y de alla* in my soul; there was no other way. The dedication and time my femtors invested in my wellness and development was vital as I transitioned through the branching stages of my life. While in college, I connected with femtors that served as staff and faculty of color in the institution and saw how they led through mothering, through self-as-example. These women gave me a glimpse into their beautifully crafted identities, one in which they interwove their race, ethnicity, class, and gender—all fluid—to lead from an authentic place. Their guidance grounded me when I felt lost, as though I did not belong either here or there. They encouraged me to explore ideas of discipline, chosen family, and leadership. Their unconditional support and love was the *leche* that sustained me and shaped me into the mothering-leader I am today: I honor them.

Having recently welcomed my daughter into this world, my understanding of mothering continues to evolve. As my *leche* changes to adapt to the needs of my daughter, equally I continue to transform the ways I interact with my communities. Rooted in the understanding of it all is not to change who I am, but rather to embrace and reimagine. Like the long nights where my *leche* continues to be a source of sustenance for my daughter. Yet she sustains me as much as I sustain her. And although I am left with emptied breasts and the cramping from my shrinking uterus, the satisfaction she experiences while being fed serves as my fuel to continue breastfeeding.

In many ways, my journey with breastfeeding has been similar to navigating US culture, where I have needed to develop the courage to believe that my milk is enough, despite not having a high milk flow, and the resilience to accept the insensitive comments, unsolicited advice, and criticism from others. Leading and mothering—*de aqui y de alla*—has allowed me to be vulnerable and do my best, with the comfort of knowing I can engage in communal mothering. I can lean on my sisters, my femtors, and use my mother's *chocolate con leche* to practice and refine these mothering-leader skills, knowing that the *leche* that comes, however it transcends/lets down, is enough. It is of many streams: We are more than we believe.

As an AfroLatinx leader mothering the communities I am part of, and come from, I am the essence of constant evolution. Even as my identity continues to shift, my values—the moral compass within me—remain constant. I have the most beautiful yet complex job, a balancing act of jumping double Dutch during the day and dancing salsa at night. While partaking in both, I accept that I am choosing to actively be in partnership with others (my daughter, co-workers, students, etc.), trusting myself to lead and also be led. My communities may need a different side of me, one that requires me to change with them as they change—*de aqui y de alla*. To be moldable, flexible, and adaptable to the metamorphosis of humanity. A constant change: A feeling of reinventing myself comes with a necessity to mother in different ways.

Being in the process of becoming is part of human nature—part of being adaptable to change; being willing to consider where I am in a given moment; the facts, and the feelings I hold; to then create the best balance of decisions possible for the communities I nurture, love, and care for. I lead by recognizing that although we are different (in that the worlds we inhabit may feel different), at our core we are *de aqui y de alla*, and I am here for it. I love my family—chosen and blood—and will continue to center their wellness with the hope of preserving their essence. Everything they have left with me has been planted within, growing through me as extensions, as spiritual vines.

Nothing is promised. But life is beautiful. With time, with the mothering around me, I have learned to use my AfroLatinidad to create rich, blended spaces where the complexities of our identities can be seen and celebrated. I strive to live and manifest authentically, in all my sides of relating, as a way to encourage others to do the same. My AfroLatinidad is majestic. My AfroLatinidad transcends category. My AfroLatinidad is as powerful as it is healing. My AfroLatinidad is the deepest source of my being as mother, as sustenance, as daughter, as I now share with my own daughter all that grows through me—and as I transform and exchange *leche* with those who have granted me the chance to lead in their spaces—my spaces, my daughter's spaces: *our* spaces.

DISCUSSION

In analyzing our *testimonios*, we were interested in finding themes that spoke to our processes of becoming AfroLatinx leaders. Each *testimonio* emphasized moments in our lives that were meaningful and consequential in shaping how we understand ourselves in the world. The process of coming into self is an important part of becoming an AfroLatinx leader. We focused on the moments where we felt ourselves being called into our leadership. That is, we did not choose leadership per se, but we understand our path to leadership as being shaped by our life circumstances and as a response to a need we witnessed—we felt/shared; we intuited—in our communities. Everytime we return to our *testimonios*, we are somewhere new. *Dando LECHE* as a heuristic came about through the process of moving through our *testimonios*—the act of seeing, recording, naming. From our writing emerged the concept of *dando LECHE*, which translates in English to "giving milk." *Dando LECHE* is a tool that helps us name the various and multiple ways our leadership praxis mirrors how we mother our families, communities, institutions, and selves toward liberation as AfroLatinx people. *LECHE* as felt memory, as spiritual transfer, as community praxis: **L**eading with love; **E**mpowering communities, each other, and ourselves; **C**ompass(ionate) guidance, **H**onoring our her/their stories; **E**xpansive and transformative praxis. We honor these five growth ways and more deeply explicate the themes below.

Leading with Love

Our *testimonios* attempt to document defining moments along our paths to becoming leaders. These moments were often shrouded in adversity, presenting as a challenge to be overcome. It was through these trials that we came to understand the kinds of leaders we wanted to be: those who lead with love. Similar to learning how to care for a child, leading with love requires active listening—knowing when to step in and when to step out. Krista describes her trials with breastfeeding and navigating other people's expectations of her body; this was a lesson in making hard decisions and sticking with them despite limited [institutional] support. As Krista describes her journey with her child and building a communal relationship with her *leche*, her belovedother teaches her how to be vulnerable as she learns to have difficult conversations in order to communicate her intentions and needs.

Roseilyn describes having an abundance of femtors that modeled being true to self while being leaders in their respective communities. This type of representation was empowering, calling Roseilyn into her leadership to replicate the love and care she received. As a foil to this, Krista writes about her fragmented connections with Black female leaders she admired. Rather than allowing these disappointments to consume her, she was motivated to reimagine the gap she experienced in these disconnections—to become a leader who is accessible, supportive, and expansive: mothering with empathy to inspire care and collective worth. All of these learnings/imaginings inform what it means to lead with love. It is both a skill and a knowing that comes through time and experience.

For both of us, being a leader means being a reflection of our communities not only in who we are and what we believe but also in how we move through the world. Positioning ourselves as both teachers and learners who lead with love, we have translated our deep connections with people into empathy as a leadership practice (Garcia, 2018). Not only are we able to relate to feelings of discrimination and othering experienced by the people we serve, we are committed to using our "influence to create opportunities to empower Black communities everywhere" (Garcia, 2018; Laurent-Perrault, 2012, p. 183). Our mothering-leadership and the *leche* that flows through allows us to imagine and create the possibilities inherent in an AfroLatinx existence which celebrates, recognizes, and unconditionally lifts us all so that we may sculpt our "in-between" (Garcia, 2018) into a mutable and real place-of-being; we live here, love here, and always will.

Empowering Communities, Each Other, and Ourselves

Empowering communities, each other, and ourselves starts with knowing and being confident in who you are. We cannot give what we do not have; a person is only able to make *leche* if they are giving their body the things it needs to sustain production. In the same vein, we cannot empower others if we ourselves are not empowered in who we are. Despite the many differences in our lived experiences, there were common threads that surfaced through our *testimonios*, a record of how we made sense of self. How people perceived us, at first, had been rooted in negative judgment, causing us to harbor feelings of *not being enough* or *being too much*—our "excess flesh" as Black Latinx women stays "troubling to dominant visual culture" (Fleetwood, 2011, p. 110). Yet our emotional read of these disconnections that we had internalized motivated us to come to a deeper understanding of who we are as people, connected to rich histories of being and thriving; we far exceed the narrow, stereotypical assumptions of what it means to be Black and Latinx. We release the systemic wavelengths which have kicked up dissonance for our people, our beautiful dynamic manifestations, and communities. We release the narratives we inadvertently inherited and/or absorbed—narratives which sometimes made us feel as though we were on islands, alone, yet, looking around the diaspora, also intensely multiple. We remember playing back cassettes of sayings, words, illogic presented as logic; these harms were/are songs that circle around a dispossession of self/selves, but they are not our own, and we release them too. We have experienced dispossession within our bodies/spirits, even as we are so visibly, audibly, feelingly present. Our bodies and presence have never been empty spaces. It is not new for our existence to frustrate the expectations of others, but they cannot erase us. As our Indigeneity and Latinidad flow through us, so we honor our nuanced and exceptional, complex and varied origins/present ways of being. We practice grace; and release—as rhythm, in movement, through breath. Music travels with us, through us, and we will shape-shift, grow love, and continue to be gateways to the rich landscapes (mosaic/mural/tapestries of memory/body/voice) we contain but can miss seeing/believing if we are not careful. We empower so no one forgets. Our expressions, our art, our study of the land and her offerings—*curandera yerbera partera* mothering-wisdom—they fill many *testimonios* beyond our own. All we have seen, felt, received, buried, blessed—found here too. These understandings travel with our *leche*, our humanity.

As the *testimonios* suggest, the work of coming into self is never complete, but a beautiful, ever-evolving process of becoming. For Krista this came in the form of spiritual awakening that rooted her in a way that "allow[ed] for agency and self-expression." Krista's recounting of her coming into Santería is a return home of sorts, a fundamental characteristic of the search for diasporic personhood, a process marked by truth, humility, and patience (Modestin, 2012). Roseilyn describes the questioning she endured from outsiders who did not have the capacity to understand who she was in all her radiance and complexity, and these questions in turn created self-doubt. Yet Roseilyn was able to find solace in the mothering she received at home and the ways her parents created a Black-affirming environment that allowed Roseilyn to be nourished and flourish in all parts of her being. These experiences ground Roseilyn and Krista in their approach to leadership and how through their *leche* they are able to harness and channel power into those with whom they share space.

In our desire to exist in our wholeness, we took the time to get to know ourselves better, educate ourselves about the past, and build out our community with folks who affirmed our ways of being. In finding power in our own intersecting identities, we became better equipped to empower others to do the same.

Compass(ionate) Guidance

What does it mean to be a compass? To guide others on their journeys? For us, mothering/caregiving, leading/guiding, compassion/intimacy become *leche*. Mothering comes from a place of profound love for life that is and is not one's own. It is through love that we connect at a spiritual level with others and find fulfillment. In this way we can understand that "there is no better compass than compassion"; as leaders we serve as a compass for others through the ways we demonstrate care in all aspects of our work (Gorman, 2021, p. 48). This type of compassionate guidance connects back to the idea of giving and getting nourished. This is exemplified in Roseilyn's description of her mother's *chocolate con leche* as "an act of love, care, and nourishment." In giving of herself by waking up early in order to leave this token of affection for her children before heading out to work, we see how milk as nourishment becomes a conduit for care. For Roseilyn, the *chocolate con leche* was more than a drink but an outward manifestation of her mother's love which gave her the "strength to survive, thrive, and find joy" in her everyday experiences. As a leader, Roseilyn seeks to replicate these feelings in the ways she interacts with others and carries out her work. Being guided by compassion and offering compassionate guidance go hand in hand.

As AfroLatinx mothers and leaders, we help guide our children and communities to engage with their full selves. Our desire to always go above and beyond—to meet everyone's needs—is sometimes framed as resilience, but it is in fact our ingenuity that has allowed us to subverse the limitations imposed by oppressive systems toward creating a lived world where we can prosper. It is in this creative process that our *leche* has shape-shifted to accommodate the evolving ways it is needed and sustained. We carry this same energy into our work outside the home, giving of ourselves in how we build relationships, approach problem-solving, and care for communities. In these and countless other ways, we model care-centered leadership, which emphasizes connecting with folks on numerous levels in order to build strong connections that form the foundation for Black people to thrive in spaces not originally designed for us, where we collectively nourish one another toward Black joy.

Honoring Our Her/Their Stories

AfroLatinx leadership is also a feminist project that is rooted in the many her/their stories that have sought out liberation. In critically engaging with our own words, we were gifted the opportunity to put our voices in conversation with other Black/Third World/radical feminists who have offered their stories for the collective intellectual, social, and political growth of Black and Brown communities. In particular, our *testimonios* breathe life into the idea of "theory in the flesh" first posited by Cherríe Moraga (1981) and since taken up by countless feminist scholars (p. 24). We add our nuanced stories to this landscape/body of her/their stories "that are likewise intellectual, political, and spiritual praxes that bring to the fore the histories, living legacies, and racialized gender dimensions of . . . multivalent oppressions" (Moraga & Anzaldúa, 1981, p. 24) (Figueroa, 2020, p. 222) while simultaneously powerfully pushing open the boundaries of Blackness to include AfroLatinx realities (Zamora, 2017). In conjuring them into this space, sharing the pages with these mothers of AfroLatinx studies, we remind the readers and ourselves of the deep-rooted traditions of Black liberation in Latinx communities in the United States and abroad. *Gracias a elles/*Thanks to them for their trailblazing leadership, which has opened doors and deepened the cornerstone of our own and countless others' leadership trajectories.

Our *testimonios* add to the living archive of AfroLatina feminist scholarship, whose scope, variation, and vision names and affirms the possibilities in AfroLatinidades through the sharing of *leche*, perspective, and open stories. In writing down our experiences, we aim to show how our stories have taken shape only because of the many other stories that came before us—our *mamás*, *abuelas*, *y tías* that sat around the kitchen table processing their days and preparing for their futures; the *activistes* that challenged systems and structures in order to build more livable worlds; the *aristes* that dreamed up new realities and offered us something to aspire for. Speaking our truths required us to be vulnerable and sit in the uncomfortable. This was particularly palpable in the sharing of our breastfeeding stories. The difficulties of breastfeeding often go unspoken because it is touted as "best practice." But it is damn hard. In having the space to voice this, we open space for others to feel okay to feel, to add variation to the common narrative, and to lean into our lived experiences. By honoring our stories we join a long list of folks who have been vanguards of their time by speaking their truths. These stories, born of the flesh, nourished our souls: the milk that fortifies us.

Expansive and Transformative Praxis

As AfroLatinx leaders, we have chosen to use our mothering skills in transformational ways, allowing us to engage our children, communities, and selves in our totality. We use our *leche* to provide love and a sense of belonging to our children as they transition from our womb to the real world, always ensuring their safety and fulfilling their physiological needs. But to see Black people as their whole selves is to focus on the development of their esteem and self-actualization as individuals and as part of our communities. To be transformative in our approach, we must teach and model prioritizing self-care, rest, and critical self-reflection to sustain this work. Additionally, we understand the power in creating spaces where folx can comfortably exist with the ambiguity and complexities of their identities. As we continue to mother in our leadership roles, we know that to be effective and trusted in our roles, we must accept and expect that our *leche* will and must change with time, just as our children/communities change. Just as the orisha have modeled, *leche* as love can manifest as stepping in/out, leaning into gentleness or firmness, sharing wisdom, or creating space for listening and growth—harnessing reciprocity.

As a praxis that is both expansive and transformative, mothering and leading are rooted in abundance thinking, which suggests that "if we develop relationships based on sharing our struggles *and* our resources, we do in fact have enough of everything—love, food, energy, and power" (Greene Brown, 2020, p. 105). In reimagining mothering and leadership as communal, rather than individual actions geared toward liberation, we develop everyday practices that are reflexive and refractive of Black power and broad, collaborative possibility. This praxis, grounded in ancestral and Indigenous knowledge forms, provides the guidance to free ourselves from normative understandings of mothering and leading (Duran, 2019). As we come, so we are: Our work is our love, our care, our *leche*—our leading, the mothering that found us—informed by the mothering which flows through us as guide.

CONCLUSION

We have used our *testimonios* to assert our AfroLatinidad in the context of Black women's leadership in higher education because we believe that widening our understanding of Black leadership to include AfroLatinx people and perspectives is essential to increasing our visibility and how we are valued in these spaces. Naming how we understand coming into ourselves and its importance in shaping how we take on and enact leadership is essential to creating more inclusive and empowering spaces for AfroLatinx leaders.

Through this labor of love, we came into ourselves as scholars contributing to the legacy of AfroLatinx leadership. A legacy that is rooted in intangible gifts such as the memories we shared, the friendship we strengthened, and the respect and love we showed each other. This process gave us the opportunity to beautifully write and intimately depict how our upbringings led us to where we are today. We found ourselves thinking back to when it all started, and we had a lot to say; this chapter allowed us to heal by *testimoniando*. Our writing took many iterations; each time we came back to our words, we learned something new and saw a different part of ourselves. The ability to sit with our words, reflect, and try things out resulted in the weaving together of meaning and moments that collapsed time/space.

Our hope is that from our *testimonios* you understand that leading and mothering cannot exist without each other. We close out this offering by encouraging you to pause and engage in self-reflection to further explore and unearth what leadership and mothering means to you. As a point of entry:

- How do we move forward as leaders and mothers in a world that is constantly asking/demanding us to change along with it?
- What beliefs and values do you want to instill in others through your leadership and mothering?
- If children are an extension of us on Earth, then what does it mean for you to leave a legacy behind?
- In what ways can you encourage others to continue growing and developing as both leaders and mothers?

Chapter 3

Beyond the Veil
The Black Girl I Could Be
DeLisha Tapscott

CHILE, BEING BLACK WOMEN AIN'T FOR THE WEARY

I am tired. No, better yet, I am exhausted. As a Black woman, consistently being expected to be "on" at all times fills my cup until it runs over with the guilt for all the things I could not get to. I am a mother. A student. A professional. A lover. A friend. A sister. A mentor. And still, I often wonder, *Who am I?* I can name all my roles for others, but I find it challenging to name myself. When I move throughout my world, I often move to benefit others. As I bend and alter my identity to fit those needs, the answer to my question feels more elusive than I could ever imagine. Imagining things feels elusive too. Dreaming beyond this code I switch into while interacting in corporate spaces feels odd. Stepping outside of myself feels normal. Not entirely step and fetch, yet not quite myself. I am exhausted, pacing up and down the halls of my virtual office, smiling. By the end of the day, my face hurts, but to drop the act threatens my livelihood and the livelihood of those I care for.

I feel I must always remain professional or risk being *othered* (Collins, 1986). I represent every Black woman who sits next to me and hopes to enter these walls. So I cannot slip or let them see me sweat. Hold it all in, breathe later, eat later, self-care later, rest later. *Rest*. I forgot what it looked like to rest. I forgot what it felt like to breathe in serenity, self-love, and breathe out the day. Sometimes I catch glimpses of it in my peripheral view. Kinda like how you catch the sleep in your eye, always in the corner, never able to catch it.

Rest has become automated, not replenishing. I eat after the kids go to bed and sleep once the work is in. When I lie in bed, I wait for my mind to calm down. Two hours have passed. I have counted my breath and listened to the rhythm of my heartbeat so much that I have caused my body to panic. Its fight-or-flight response engulfs me as I watch my loved ones enjoying sleep peacefully. I use apps to distract my body from panicking because I cannot lull my body back into a calm space. I refuse medicines because I am already on blood pressure and water pills to keep me from having a heart attack like my mom. I am fearful of that. This reminds me to see the doctor next month and schedule a call with my therapist while I'm at it. I wish I could have more time there, but I value my roles for others more than keeping myself sane. But who am I keeping sane?

Furthermore, why does it feel like I am carrying my entire tribe on my back? I feel like I cannot let down the others. I cannot stop feeling lost. I cannot stop looking for answers. I cannot stop feeling exhausted. The balancing act of personal and professional often overlaps and impacts how I show up within settings that do not center my identity. When I enter my office, though virtual, imagine you see me sitting in front of a screen. While I seemingly look alone, I am ultimately carrying the weight of those who came before me, those who depend on me, those who will one day enter this space, and those impacted by what the space produces. Within work culture, it is easy to think linearly about how identity plays a part in our interaction with one another. However, literature repeatedly notes that Black women often operate within structures of whiteness as hostages of the expectations of the dominant, often White, culture (McCluney et al., 2021; Rabelo et al., 2021). In addition, holding a leadership position where we internalize the often-unspoken expectation to outperform, overachieve, and provide insight into marginalized experiences often heightens our visibility within these spaces. Ultimately, where we seek transformative and lasting change through agency and autonomy, we, in many cases, are silenced and excluded though placed in positions that are sought to provide expertise to hold the organization accountable (Chance, 2022; Cyr et al., 2021).

I share my story and the dimension of my experience extensively because who I am as a leader directly correlates with who I am outside of and beyond that role. While my experiences are not monolithic, they mirror how many Black women in leadership roles are impacted by their work (Chance, 2022; Hall et al., 2011; Parker, 2001). Within this piece, I reflect on my experiences as a leader in diversity, equity, inclusion, and belonging. I dissect moments that impart knowledge surrounding performative action and its correlation with expectations for change, agency, and authority within leadership as a Black woman and the need for resistance through rest. I hope that through reading and reflecting on this writing, Black women employed in leadership positions feel validated and reflected in ways that mirror their own experiences while calling for action through resistance to enable a reconstruction of their identities within the leadership space.

SO LET ME SPEAK: A NARRATIVE

My Roots and Understanding

When I was younger, I used to go to my mom's office and help around to make a few extra bucks. Copying pages, answering the phone, labeling folders, just small tasks. I remembered watching how my mother walked around her firm. She was the office manager, overseeing everything from invoicing, answering phones, keeping the cabinets stocked, and making appointments for the lawyers. I always felt like I wanted to be her when I grew up. I wanted to wear the shoulder-padded blazer with the matching skirt, the short Anita Baker mushroom hairdo, and the earrings and walk confidently. I felt like she had it all together, and although I knew nothing about office management or law firms, I knew my path was clear. I would be working somewhere in somebody's organization, running things with my head held high, feeling like I was needed in the world around me.

As the years went by, I was often reminded that my first understanding of being powerful came from the image of my mother. In a world of whiteness, I saw her use the skills she had learned from the women before her to show up in spaces with power. While she did not hold the same power as the owners, all White and all lawyers, there was something about her role and responsibilities that gave her a level of autonomy I had never seen. So much so that when they closed, they worked hard to find her another place of employment. Those moments of seeing my mother "running the office" helped me imagine and ultimately fantasize about having the same experiences she had.

Now, as an adult, I understand how much of herself my mother had to balance working in White-dominant organizations throughout the years. Everything she did to work there was ultimately subject to the requirement that she blend into the employment environment, from how she dressed to how she spoke. She ironed her clothes every night, was always on time, worked hard even on weekends during busy seasons, and bent her back to the will of her environment. Looking back on it, I understand how important it was for her to teach me how to "play the game" to survive a world that saw me as an outsider within its walls (Collins, 1986). When I was younger, her favorite thing to say was "It is what it is." Child me was not able to understand the severity of that statement. I was not able to separate the moments of anguish my mother felt. Instead, I focused on the power she held when she stepped foot through those office doors as I completely ignored the moments when her Blackness and womanhood impacted her.

Looking back, I remember when my mother sat on the edge of the bed, not wanting to go to work. I remember how slowly she moved to get ready at 6:30 a.m. every morning. I remember when she came home in tears after a lawyer yelled and cursed at her for a simple mistake. I remember my father having to come to her job to show them that she was not alone and had someone there to protect her from such moments. As I got older, I asked my mother about her experiences. I hoped to understand if it was worth it all. Was it worth it when the White folks at her job would not treat her respectfully and underpay her? Was it worth it to hold back her emotions and sigh, understanding that this was the world she lived in? My mother would tell you it was not, but it was all she knew. Her mother had not worked in an office before her. She had been a maid and child caretaker, never working in an office. What she learned, she learned on her own and through her own understanding of how the world works around her. My mother, who will soon be 70, has lived through so much of this world. She was 9 years old when affirmative action laws were enacted, 11 when the Birmingham church was bombed, 12 when Jim Crow laws ended, 15 when Dr. King was assassinated, 40 when the L.A. riots happened, and is now 69 amid the Black Lives Matter movement.

My mother has lived life, and her perception of her positionality within environments built to center whiteness came with an understanding that she only made it there by the skin of her teeth. She did not have the agency or the wherewithal to shift the narratives of the organizations. She worked because her purpose was to make money to clothe and feed her family, which was more important to her than being mistreated at work. As an adult, I have often thought back on her experiences and wondered how my own understanding of agency has impacted how I have had to show up in spaces of whiteness.

Thinking back on the unspoken and often internalized behavior that seeped into my psyche, I can see the pieces of my mother I kept. I straightened my hair for a long time, thinking it would allow me to be more palatable. Being a darker-skinned Black woman, I internalized the need to coat my words in ways that erased any ounce of aggression. As a leader in the space of diversity, equity, inclusion, and belonging, I walk the line of bringing authenticity to my work and understanding the moments where my reviews or agency are viewed as a threat. In this space, I have been called upon to address the things that impact those marginalized—those without a voice. At the same time, I find that in this space there can be so many moments of focus on corrective action that there does not leave much balance for a collective and liberatory design. I often wonder if I am just here as a *talking head* or someone viewed as having expertise in spaces that matter. If, ultimately, the work I push forward gets rejected by those in power, am I truly leading, or am I following those who lead me in directions I do not seek to go?

Deep into Work: Who I Am

When I think about how I started this work, I am reminded that there was no direct line to diversity, equity, and inclusion. If you ask me why I decided to make this work my life, I would tell you it was a combination of bad bosses, Sandra Bland, and Black women. I separate Sandra Bland from Black women because her murder marked a change for me. Nevertheless, before that moment, I felt like there had been moments throughout my life where I felt the pressure of inequity sitting on my chest, making it harder to breathe. I often think about the early points in my childhood that began to lay the foundation for shifting my consciousness. I often ask myself which instance caused my young mind to begin to see this world differently. In which instance did my Blackness hit head-on with the biases of this country? As a young Black girl from southeast DC and brought up in the Blackest county in Maryland, Prince George's County, I had always been surrounded by Blackness. Being from "chocolate cities," my perception of my Blackness being a positive thing was high. I saw myself in the students, teachers, and city, so there has always been a feeling of home. While at home, I felt encouraged and supported; however, when I ventured out of that setting, I noticed that I felt more and more out of place.

When I finally stepped into this work, I was in my late 20s. I finally decided my path in this world was organizational management, specializing in the nonprofit sector. I truly fell in love with it. I fell in love with making an impact at an organization's core. See, I believe that an organization's narrative was created at the center of the people. Want to change the organization? Listen to the people. I quickly realized that folks with power substituted listening to the people for the projections they had about people. The content of their "knowing" occurred without an effort to know the inner experience of others. They only listened in the proximity of how they understood the organization. Regardless of how much the organization claimed that equity mattered or that they made decisions with the people in mind, behind closed doors—and sometimes out in the open—they made decisions that were often in the company's interest. Sometimes those interests ran counter to the experiences of the people. In these instances, I found that these decisions were made in the interest of the organization's dominant culture—in other words, the White folks. Is it surprising? Not really, not considering that the companies I have worked for have all been White-dominant organizations. However, the one thing that has always stood out to me is that within these organizational management positions, that is, human resources, people operations, diversity, equity, and inclusion roles, Black women led the charge of this work. For me, I always wonder why.

The Category Is . . . Black Women

What drew them to these roles? Was there a sense of comfort or validation that these companies felt in hiring them for these positions? Were they promised an equitable utopia, flexibility, the ability to hold the company accountable, and the power to lead how they saw fit? Furthermore, if they were, how soon did they realize it was all a ruse? What was their breaking point. Which policy rejection, microaggression, or dismissive behavior woke them up to the reality that while they were leaders in the title, they were not considered leaders with the freedom to lead? For me, it is the moments when I am forced to change how I respond to things impacting staff because senior leadership is set in its ways. It is also those moments where we center whiteness in equity conversations and then get called *too Black* and not *inclusive enough*. My favorite is when the number of BIPOC employees begin to quit and no one bats an eye to finding out why. Those are the moments where I question myself as a leader, the moments that make me question if I authentically belong in spaces like these.

Honestly, I do not think I have ever called myself a DEIB (Diversity, Equality, Inclusion, and Belonging) practitioner. Instead, I understand that I am a person who is impassioned about standing with those who are not included in the discussion but are expected to accept the outcomes of what is decided. I would also describe myself as someone who found this work because Black women laid the foundation. Moreover, even though I have spent most of this work without the necessary education, I have always felt an affinity when in this space. I have existed within White spaces that seek to proclaim themselves as equitable, including those that work to make things equitable for marginalized communities in various fields, including education, politics, and healthcare. Each of these organizations had taken on the task of making things equitable for "all" without really understanding just how inequitable their idea of "all" was. They chose approaches internally designed for their environments based on their identity markers and experiences they understood. They fought tooth and nail against practices that would actually move the needle on change and gleefully accepted things that presented nicely. This is not to say they got it wrong all the time; however, when it mattered, when it came to losing Black, Brown, and Indigenous voices, they often ignored the collective narrative for their enclosed understanding.

Throughout my 17 years of work experience, I have primarily worked in operations roles, either administrative or human resources functions. During that time, the one thing that remained constant was Black women leading the work. Black women leading this work but hitting a concrete ceiling regarding decision-making. I found that Black women were giving their all, telling their organizations what needed to happen, and that expertise was falling on deaf ears. In addition, as a Black female leader, I have found that Black women have been tasked with fixing the white supremacy characteristics of an organization but have not always been given the freedom to run without the limits of White fragility. That fragility has many of them negotiate themselves, bend in spaces where they would fight back, and mentor other Black women in ways that limit their ability to show up as authentically as they should be (McCluney & Rabelo, 2019). As a Black woman, I remember starting out falling into the trap of negotiating myself by changing my hair to something more *professional*, shortening my name because it was too hard to say, conforming to body stereotypes, and changing my style of dress to make others more comfortable. As a leader of equity work, I have had to acknowledge that that negotiation impacted my mental health and thus needed to stop. In that understanding, I have attempted to reenter this work as authentically as possible. Has that kept me out of specific spaces? Yes. Has that made others uncomfortable and thus helped label me as problematic and outspoken? Absolutely. However, I realized I could not sacrifice my sanity, belief system, or calling to stand with the underrepresented for those uncomfortable with where it will take them. In that realization, I understand that to exist in this work, I have to be able to save myself from self-destruction and burnout.

What Is Required? Silence, Confusion, and Exclusion

My role in and of itself seems simple enough. My purpose is to work in community to design structures of resistance against oppression by asking the right questions. Is this equitable? Have we included a diverse group of perspectives? Have we consulted the impacted community? Have we thought about how this feels for those with marginalized intersecting identities? So on and so on. Most days, I feel like I am making progress—actually, that is a lie. Most days, I wonder what in hell I am doing here. Is this helping? Am I moving the needle and helping folks combat the whiteness? Or am I just using buzzwords to feel good about myself? I swear, if equity work had a drinking game component, I would be in the hospital for all the times *embedding* and *equity* come up in everyday language.

Often, I feel stuck. I wonder if I am helping the impacted people in my organization or making it worse. Do the various trainings, advisory teams, and policy changes mean anything to their day-to-day lives within these organizations, or am I helping to feed into White fragility? When I push back, I am often met with resistance in the form of microaggressions in the hopes of getting the uppity negro off her soapbox. Often, I feel tired. I sit in spaces of whiteness, wondering why the weight of creating an environment of inclusivity sits on the shoulders of the Black women with the title. Is it not a group effort? Furthermore, if my development of trainings and advisory teams does not work, why do I suspect I will be the only one burned at the stake? AND!

If I am the only one on trial, why in hell am I setting myself up? This work is not for the weary. This work is not for the easily impacted or those looking for a cookie. When I get the wins, I live to fight another day; when I lose, I get blamed for the losses, which means I walk around with what feels like a scarlet letter on my back. That letter indicates the score of my trustworthiness in the eyes of whiteness. It questions my moves with each newly deemed "mistake," and their doubt in me grows. That doubt spreads across the organization like wildfire, inviting those without education or life experience to suddenly have expertise over what was once deemed my domain. Ultimately it has me questioning my purpose and intentions and begs the question, "Am I here for the people or to uphold the dominant narrative?"

While I write this not to deter others from this work, I seek to remove any ability to gravitate toward rose-colored utopian vibes. They do not exist within this work. There are often no rewards for this work; in many ways, the "thank-yous" given in one breath are often negated in the next due to those within the organization reverting to their routine behaviors. I do not do this work for myself and myself alone. Instead, I do this work *with* the people without the power to sit in the rooms I do to breathe life and to tell their narratives. I do this work for those who tense up in spaces not created to enjoy the sound of their voices. I do this work for those who shoot me a glance that tells me, "Sista girl, keep fighting." I do it for the people who exist uncomfortably within these spaces that rely on White comfort.

For that, I beg of you, the reader, to find your why. My why is undoubtedly the love I have for Black women. They are the foundation of why I do this work. It does not mean that I do not seek to make changes for other impacted individuals. Instead, it means my narrative exists to uphold the voices of Black women. I exist in these spaces as a Black woman, which pushes me forward in this work above all else. If the pandemic has taught me nothing else in doing this work, it is that whiteness spreads quicker behind the internet wall. The addition of remote work due to COVID-19 has allowed microaggressions to show up more frequently without much conscious effort. They become second-nature attacks that do more than sting as they land. To create shifts in this work for practitioners and organizations and resist this organizational culture, be analyzed. The narratives and expertise of Black women leaders must rise to the top of the organizations that hire them.

METHODOLOGY AND FRAMING: GROUNDED IN THE EXPERTISE OF BLACK WOMEN

When deciding to embark on the journey of writing this piece, I contemplated the methodology that would give this work meaning and the epistemological approaches that would shape the framing of this work. I utilize Black feminist autoethnography to explore my personal experiences as a Black female leader and how they connect to the cultural experience of other Black women leaders within the literature (Ellis et al., 2011). I ground my experience in the theoretical frameworks of intersectionality (the lens) and the cultural contracts theory, while the conditions of visibility help to contextualize the circumstances that influence the agency of Black women leaders.

Black Feminist Autoethnography

Using autoethnography is an intentional approach I use to capture and analyze my experiences and understand the cultural experiences of Black women leaders. While qualitative in its roots, autoethnography is more than just a few autobiographical narratives. Autoethnography conceptualizes autobiographical narratives within the theoretical frame of a discipline to provide transformative learning and understanding of the phenomenon (Custer, 2014; Ellis & Bochner, 2006). Coupled with the Black feminist perspective, autoethnography provides an intersectional viewpoint of the systemic structures (e.g., sexism, racism, classism) that impact the lens of Women of Color. This methodological approach permits critical self-analysis and reflexivity in a way that cedes power from the dominant narratives of the environment back into the hands of those who experience oppression within their environment. In this case, Black feminist autoethnography allows Black women researchers to look inward at themselves and then turn their lens back toward their environment to connect their personal experiences to larger cultural experiences (Boylorn, 2008).

Collins's (2000) Black feminist thought focuses on the suppression of Black women within the White patriarchal controlled institutions that reinforce the subjugation of Black women from expressing their ideas, experiences, and consciousness. Black feminist thought allows Black women to construct their consciousness by utilizing their tools, including language, art, and community. Taking into account the multilayered and intricate experiences of Black women, we realize that by writing ourselves into the plot, our histories and lens on the world around us warp the assertive narrative of our oppressors.

Focusing on my story allows me to humanize my experiences and find a place for the internalizations that have imprinted themselves within me due to the environment I have existed in. Through autoethnography, I was able to utilize this method as a resource of critical-reflexive discourse that allows me to express the intersections between my culture and my identity and moves beyond my personal experiences into the cultural experiences of societal structures that provide context to how Black women have been socialized

(Spry, 2001). In the spaces that seek to silence and penalize the voices of Black women, autoethnography combined with Black feminism seeks to liberate and resist by pushing against those boundaries in the hopes of moving the narrative away from the margin to the center (Collins, 2000; Crenshaw, 1990; Shorter-Gooden, 2004).

Framing This Narrative

To tell my story is one thing, but to blend in with it, the supportive literature means that my narrative must be guided by frameworks that allow for a continuous flow of storytelling. Therefore, I had to find ways to incorporate literature that grounded this work in the voices of Black folx. My experience, first and foremost, incorporates the intersectionality of my womanhood and Blackness. The two cannot be separated; therefore, my lens leans on the works of Kimberlé Crenshaw, who uses intersectionality to denote the "various ways in which race and gender interact to shape the multiple dimensions of Black women's employment experiences" (Crenshaw, 1990). Within this concept of intersectionality, we find Black women, like myself, who have been hired in a space centered on accountability of marginalized voices, who are often boxed into and excluded from truly tapping into liberatory ways that shape and shift their environments (Dickens et al., 2019; Rosser-Mims, 2010).

Taking on roles that center on diversity, equity, inclusion, and belonging amid the continuous outcries of police brutality in the United States, the rising discrimination within organizations, and internal organizational factors comes at a price for Black women as leaders and employees. Internally, Black women are faced with committing to the cultural contracts of their environments that ask them to adapt or assimilate to their needs while placing them on the margins (Jackson, 2002; Lamsam, 2014). This ultimately impacts how they construct their identities to combat the conditions (environment) their visibility holds on how much agency they are given within their role (Brewer, 1999; Crenshaw, 1989; Dickens et al., 2019; McCluney & Rabelo, 2019).

Therefore, the cultural contracts theory (CCT) introduced by Jackson (2002) supports the description of Black women's environment by touching on negotiating their identities to reduce conflicts that arise as a result of their undetachable identities. It notes that Black women utilize the concept of negotiation as a strategy to construct an identity for the workplace and one that exists externally (Jackson, 2002; Ting-Toomey, 2015). This theory frames how Black women conform to negotiation as a coping mechanism within spaces that do not empower or uplift their authority and expertise. This theory also explores an understanding that each person walks into a workplace environment signing an invisible contract to participate in exchanging pieces of their identity to gain acceptance from the dominant culture (Jackson, 2002). However, when analyzed to include cultural expression of intersecting identities, the cultural contracts theory suggests that conflict may arise for Black women because they have unerasable identities associated with their race and gender. They cannot detach themselves from their Blackness or their womanhood (Lamsam, 2014). Therefore, their Blackness and womanhood act as double jeopardy and further *others* them within spaces where power imbalances exploit and intensify their experiences (Collins, 2000; Jackson & Harris, 2007).

To finally frame my narrative, I use the conceptual framework of McCluney and Rabelo (2019) called the Conditions of Visibility (CoV) to define the circumstances surrounding how and why Black women exist in these environments. Within my narrative, I focus on how my visibility, aligned with my agency and autonomy, intersects with how a culture of whiteness within the organization I worked within undermined the holistic inclusion of me as a Black woman, which ultimately informed my need to resist and repair to maintain my well-being.

The Intersection of Autoethnography and the Frameworks

To gather my thoughts, I needed to visually understand how these things connect to my narrative. This piece initiates the formulation of what a more radical and unapologetic resistance looks like to combat the veil I have been wearing. That thought sits at the center of this because I hope by honestly sharing my experiences, they will validate the experiences of others. The focus of this topic is necessary to cultivate space and an understanding of how to lead more authentically in spaces that call for Black women's greatness through overperformance and fixing broken systems (per the Drake quote) but that do not provide Black women with the autonomy to lead in ways authentic to ourselves (Brewer, 1999; Rabelo et al., 2021; Shorter-Gooden, 2004). Utilizing narrative will allow for a focus on where I have been, who I would like to become, and what I need to achieve it. Ultimately, it seeks to answer the following question:

What kind of leader could Black women become if given full agency to exist unapologetically as themselves?

Holding the identity of a Black woman, I use a layered account of my experiences that explores my stream of consciousness, tapping into how I see the world and how I show up within it (Ronai, 1996). My story, like many, seeks to invoke, inspire, and provide validation to other Black women leaders and their experiences. It invites them to examine their own internalizations about the environments they have existed in and how they impact their feelings surrounding their agency and leadership abilities. Lastly, while I cannot speak on behalf of all Black women, I hope my thoughts on how to radically and unapologetically resist these oppressions guide them to find their own ways of resistance (see figure 3.1).

Black Women, White Spaces

Rabelo et al. (2021) analyzed whiteness through the practice of the white gaze and how Black women are impacted by it. The purpose of the study was to understand how whiteness marginalizes those that are not aligned with its narrative. Utilizing Twitter (now X), they created a hashtag, #BlackWomenAtWork, to identify the mechanisms that whiteness perpetuated Black women's bodies through critical discourse analysis. Their main focus was to look into the experiences of Black women and how they interact with the concept of the White gaze within the workplace. Surveying through Twitter garnered them 1,169 eligible tweets; they found that Black women are often being forced, conditioned, and controlled by the White gaze. The White gaze, through embodiment, impacts the power relations within these spaces and maintains racist structures through the regulation and punishment of Black women's bodies (Rabelo et al., 2021). What can be implied by this study is that Black women, through the creation of an organizational cross-complacency, maintain and uphold racism at the expense of Black women.

In addition, Jean-Marie et al. (2009) discuss Black women in leadership and how stereotypes, biases, racism, and sexism intersect how they lead. It also looks at how race and gender impact how they inclusively develop their leadership style and build consensus and collaboration. As other studies have

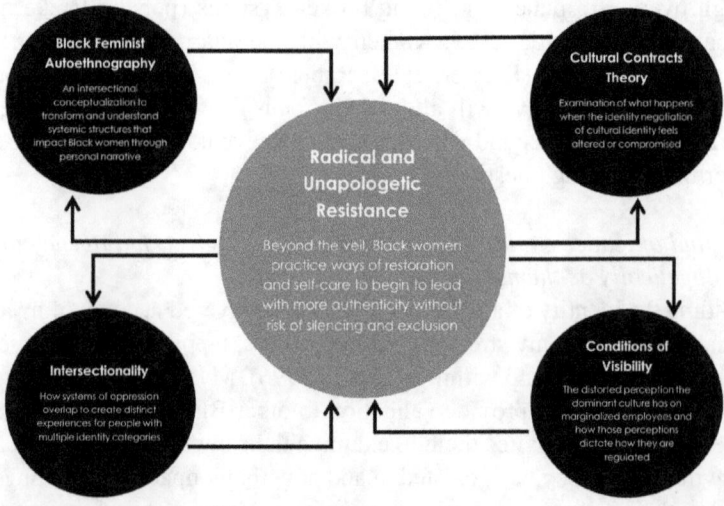

Figure 3.1 Toward a More Radical Elsewhere

mentioned, the concept of double jeopardy impacts Black women's navigation within the workplace. At the same time, unrelenting challenges and discrimination create a glass-ceiling effect in which they cannot transcend barriers to an organization's upper levels of leadership. The data suggest that Black women's experiences are varied, but that they share similar encounters with institutional patterns of racism and sexism. It also suggests that due to discrimination over time, many of these women are the first in their families to attain higher levels of education. They build social capital and resiliency to create change through their leadership positions, even while combating bias (Jean-Marie et al., 2009).

What can be understood about the above is that as Black women exist and, in some cases, lead in White spaces, there is an overall impact on their physical health and their sense of wellness. The importance of marrying both their Blackness and womanhood together is advanced with the understanding that they cannot exist separately (Collins, 2000). Therefore, it is imperative that as Black women look to activate their agency within these organizations, they also set up holistic approaches that help them dream beyond the veil and work toward the possibility of leading with authenticity.

A RADICAL PLACE FOR UNAPOLOGETICALLY RESISTING

I believe that Black women have the right to live life out loud—a life inclusive of all their moments of worry, confidence, energy, solemnness, and quiet spaces—that Black women should live radically in the lessons that make up their leadership abilities. The lessons that were taught by their grandmothers, mothers, sisters, aunts, and cousins. Lessons that cannot be learned in any book or taught in any class. I believe that Black women should have the agency to self-love to heal from spaces that place them on pedestals filled with high expectations as they nip at their heels; that Black women should be allowed to tap into both their Blackness and womanhood to help them lead authentically and powerfully in their own ways. Therefore, I often wonder, if Black women leaders seize full agency, what acts of self-kindness are necessary to create a path of freedom grounded in restoration, realization, and resistance?

Freedom Is Created Through Love

When I think about what freedom looks like, I am reminded of bell hooks's notion that love is necessary for liberation (hooks, 2021). She focuses her attention on the fact that liberatory action can be crafted through love in a way that creates wholeness. Based on that notion, love is the resistance to ultimately combating systems of oppression. Understanding that helps guide me to ways to protect myself as I navigate through spaces not built for me. When I thought through what I need as a leader, as a Black woman, I immediately thought of love and what it means to love myself—loving myself as I walk through unchartered territory; loving myself in spaces where white supremacy culture is at the center. Immediately I thought of my body and how much damage I take doing this work—the moments when I do not eat, when I lose sleep, when I do not stretch, when I do not rest. Those are moments when I do not love myself. Those are the moments when I bend to oppressive environments filled with expectations, pedestals, and uneven paths.

When I take a moment to breathe in restoration and balance, I can reconcile who I am, who I need to be to continue this work, and what I need to be free. Through this understanding, I realize that this work is a movement embedded in social justice—that my well-being is vital to destroying white supremacy culture and its impacts on my body, mind, and soul. What can be understood is that there must be a revisioning of myself as a Black woman within leadership to tap into the power that exists in my leadership abilities. Through this, freedom can be crafted with love at the center and the understanding that there is no space for a one-size-fits-all. There must be moments of uniqueness, communion, and healing.

The poem "Now I Lay Me Down: Rest as Resistance" by Lucille Clifton (1993) encompasses this understanding of the importance of celebrating yourself, the day, and the ability to move forward into the light: "Won't you celebrate with me / what I have shaped into." Above, I shared this notion of freedom being rooted in love and how important it is to build a space for yourself that heals and supports you. This is no more apparent than in the last lines of the poem, which mention this notion of celebrating regardless of what has tried to kill you: "Come celebrate. . . . Something has tried to kill me/and has failed."

Every day as a Black woman, I face something that seeks to take me out of my element, take me away from knowing the greatness inside of me. Nevertheless, every day I take a moment to celebrate what I have accomplished because my ancestors could never have wished for this. When I began this piece, I asked: *What kind of leader could Black women become if given full agency to exist unapologetically as themselves?* If agency were mine to decide how to lead, I would choose to lead from my roots of understanding, from the lessons of those before me; and I would lead loudly. I would lead with my whole heart in this work. I would speak to the mountains and never stop pushing the narratives of those left behind. I would advocate without the risk of losing. I would celebrate each and every day by incorporating rest into my routine to restore my faith.

With my left hand over my right, I would enter the morning with deep breaths. I would center myself with nature by incorporating ways to move my body and practice moments of mindfulness. I would turn off my thoughts of doubt and wonder and turn on thoughts of acceptance and pause (Hersey, 2023). I would pause because I would know that when it was time to turn back to the world of doing, I would be prepared to speak life, and my resistance to oppression would feel less like the bending of my body and more like the waves of the ocean. Powerful. Necessary. Replenishing. That is what my leadership looks like, and I will never stop pushing for what is elsewhere to become present to become the Black girl I could be.

Chapter 4

Refueling

Black Women Leaders Manifesting African Warrior Queenship

Norka Blackman-Richards

Black women have been typecast and stereotyped for centuries—from "Mammy" to the "welfare mother," to the "angry Black woman." We have endured derogatory terms, tropes, and labels from imposed legacies of racism and sexism (Mgadmi, 2009). We walk into a room and the hue of our skin, the style of our hair, the sway of our hips, our sense of fashion, most things about us can elicit downgraded prejudgment (Asare, 2020). We sit at tables and our insights and contributions can be tokenized, ignored, or erased. Some find our ability to innovate and to problem-solve threatening (Asare, 2020). The brilliance of our powers is often misunderstood. Yet, as Black women, we have learned to use these powers to navigate, to survive, and to thrive. These powers are also the tools of our resistance. As Collins (2000) suggests, "When an individual Black woman's consciousness concerning how she understands her everyday life undergoes change, she can become empowered. Such a consciousness may stimulate her to embark on a path of personal freedom" (p. 10).

Poet Audre Lorde (2000) explains this: "The Black woman's place of power within each of us, is neither white nor surface; it is dark, it is ancient, and it is deep" (p. 248).

The powers of Black womanhood are thus inevitable; they run in our DNA. These ancestral powers are channeled through the immense capacity that Black women have displayed for centuries to defy the odds against all prognostications (Blackman-Richards et al., 2023). Mary McLeod Bethune stated it best: "For I am my Mother's daughter, and the drums of Africa still beat in my heart" (Williams, 2008, p.11). We glean these powers from our ancestors, our grandmothers, mothers, and aunts. They are our birthright—*our African Warrior Queenship*.

The stories of African warrior queens Amanirenas, Nzinga, and Nanny (Pitchon, 2022) serve as illustration and inspiration. History tells us that each one of these queens was victorious in either resisting conquest, forming strategic alliances, or leading troops into battle—all actions that guaranteed the freedom of their people. This is the reason the practice of re-memorializing is critical to our survival. Re-memorializing requires us to not only take note of actions but also reenact these actions within our context. Re-memorialization can serve as our fuel as we glean strength and courage from our ancestors. Through the act of re-memorializing, we are forced to investigate our past to find lessons that we can incorporate in the present, while empowering ourselves to act in the present for the future (Coleman, 2008). Our experiences as Black women leaders who must fight systems and structures that were not intended for our upliftment but rather our exclusion is not far removed from the stories or the choices of these female warriors. These queens risked their own lives and that of their people; we have risked our livelihoods, promotions, and opportunities to sit at tables, or to open doors for other women.

An illustration from pop culture of how re-memorialization of and by Black women can also be used to break barriers is the movie *The Woman King*, starring Viola Davis as Nanishka. The movie made its debut in September 2022. Set in the 1820s, *The Woman King* is a historical epic of the Agojie, the all-female warriors of the 17th century, who were the army for the West African Kingdom of Dahomey until the 19th century. The backlash against the movie, which surpassed its $50 million production cost, has been largely around the belief that the movie's depiction is faulty, and that it glorifies a tribe largely responsible for the surrendering of Africans into the hands of Europeans for the transatlantic slave trade. Actress Lupita Nyong'o was originally slated to be in the film, but in 2019 she filmed a documentary based on her own research of the Agojie in Benin. Here she discovered the Agojie's role in the slave trade. "I came here looking for the real reasons to admire them, and they really come across to me now as both heroes and victims" (Nyong'o, 2020, 45:10). One scholar, however, refuses to criticize the film, calling *The Woman King* a "love letter to our ancestors and to Black women of all generations" (Walker, 2022, para. 3). The criticism of the film, its actors—mostly dark-skinned Black women, a rare occurrence in Hollywood—and producers serves as further illustration of what Black women endure in the professional and public arenas.

On the other hand, thousands of Black women in the diaspora, all over the world, flocked to their local theaters to see *The Woman King*. The movie gave Black women permission to re-memorialize, as thousands have expressed feeling a rush of empowerment and validation after watching the movie. The movie has served as fuel for many Black women moviegoers. In a recent interview on *Etalk*, when asked why she believes the movie and her character are promoting such visceral emotions, Viola Davis (2022) stated,

> I believe so many women are putting themselves in the story. We've been sidelined, we've been gaslighted. Women's health, our bodies have been placed in secondary positions, especially Black women. And the fact that we are doing a movie that is empowering and humanizing. . . . It's making people feel less alone and making them tap into their warrior fuel. (02:16)

The Woman King broke barriers by characterizing Black womanhood in a never-before-seen light in Hollywood; most importantly, it refueled the powers that Black women have always known they possess.

THE INGREDIENTS TO OUR SUPERPOWERS

Beyond their skin, hair, and flair, Black women often walk into spaces with a mystique that is mostly feared and rarely revered. It is sometimes misread as overconfidence, all-knowingness, or an otherworldly sense of self. However, it is the intersections of our identities that are our superpowers; those identities are the connecting blocks upon which that unique sense of self is built. Black, African, Caribbean, Latina, female, immigrant, middle-aged, and cisgender are the fixings to the stew of my complex identity. Like many of my sisters who inhabit the vast diaspora, I recognize that all parts of our unique identities are the ingredients to our superpowers. When misunderstood our powers will face microaggressions, micro-insults, and micro-invalidations (Sue, 2010) in private and public arenas. These powers often immediately identify us as leaders, even when we may not have the role or carry the title. The potent aftereffects of these powers are that Black women leaders often possess this strong sense of self that permeates our work (Curtis, 2014) and provides the gravitas for us to persist.

The concept of intersectionality provides more than a theoretical foundation for the multiple identities we harbor as Black women (Crenshaw, 1989). Our intersecting identities—our superpowers—are at the core of who we are and how we perform in professional roles. These superpowers are steeped in our consciousness. We know what we are up against, and the expectations that come with these barriers, yet we often find capacity to assert ourselves and push against them. These superpowers are often manifested in our decisions, practices, and outcomes as leaders. Traditional notions of the ideal leader reinforce which bodies and identities are more desirable and capable (i.e., White, heterosexual, able-bodied men). These notions would want to pressure Black women leaders to perform to fit those identities (McCluney

& Rabelo, 2019). Yet Black women leaders working at predominantly White institutions must re-create and rewrite their own rules of leadership. We must become self-defined and self-determining within "intersecting oppressions" (Collins, 2000, p. 12). This self-definition and self-determination are a charge to, as Collins (2000) puts it, "actively grapple with the central questions facing US Black women as a collectivity" (p. 9). Thus, we should never stop questioning.

Often untold and uncelebrated is the fact that Black women have always walked paths of resistance using fearless self-definition and self-determination. Black women have rarely allowed others to box them in. In American history we see Black women stepping in and coalescing during some of the most challenging times of racial struggle, often organizing female auxiliaries to the fraternal orders of their male counterparts. Untold is the story of the Washing Society in Atlanta, which in 1881 staged a strike organizing thousands of women and men in Atlanta for higher wages for washerwomen and setting an example for other labor movements (Hunter & Kelley, 2022, 43:59). Then there was the Colored Women's League, also established in the 1800s; the National Federation of Afro-American Women; and the National Association of Colored Women (Brooks, 2018; Gates et al., 2022, 47:12). These coalitions founded, organized, and managed by Black women, served as liberatory spaces for educating, networking, and organizing. These coalitions were engaged in institution-building, focused on a Black women's agenda that consisted of uplifting the lives of Black women. Black women leaders of these organizations, such as Dorothy Height and Mary Church Terrell, took up space as de facto leaders of these organizations for years. Their leadership style and positionality often caused stratification between the same Black women they sought to empower. Mary Church Terrell saw women as naturally attentive to the needs of the afflicted and thus socially obligated to fill the needs of these (Kinsler, 2010). Dorothy Height, on the other hand, supported the argument that "Black women's focus ought to be the uplift of Black men" (Kinsler, p. 75). She believed that in order to "save the Black race" (p. 48), Black women needed to step into more subservient roles that would allow Black men to be the natural leaders. Both women, products of their generations, forwarded notions that tied to Black women's advancement was the need to be in servitude of someone else.

While applauding the groundbreaking moves of these Black women leaders, we recognize that they felt forced to fit into the social molds that would make them and their causes more palatable, more acceptable to the status quo. Often, the particularities of our intersecting identities as Black women do not seem to take major precedence, as they may be viewed as a singular or expendable issue. The divide-and-conquer strategies of colonialism are applicable even today, as Black women's issues may only be viewed from the lens of gender or race but not both, or in inclusivity of those who differ in gender or age but who stand with us on the intersecting lines of injustice.

> Liberation cannot become a reality as long as people within our communities are discriminated against, as long as they are depressed and suppressed and oppressed. In fact, we must be able to move beyond those single issues to develop a real liberation for all. (Grant, 2014, 8:53)

In history, African warrior queens took the decision to fight for the liberation of all their people. They decidedly chose to be seen and heard by not focusing on what others thought or following the social norms that would try to keep them down. Instead, they focused on what needed to be done to secure freedom.

WARRIOR FUEL FOR LIBERATORY WORK

Down through the ages, Black women have manifested their African women queenship as fearlessness in the face of obstacles. Consistently, they have exemplified the courage and willingness to confront any enemy to achieve an intended goal (Blackman-Richards et al., 2023). Our leadership as Black women will often manifest the full glory of this African warrior queenship in critical moments. In moments when it may seem that we are rendered invisible, silent, lone, and isolated voices (Curtis, 2017), we become a cohesive force to fight injustice, to bring people together, to initiate and promote healing. These are the moments that require us to become the voice of reckoning—to organize the collective, lead the march, grab a bullhorn, or take to our writing devices and provide defining and determining responses to injustice. These moments will intersect with indignation, as well as fear. At these crossroads we have two choices: *step back*, cosign to the erasure, and let oppression run its usual course; or take a drink from our warrior fuel, *step in* under unwanted spotlights, and draw the line for justice. The latter is liberatory work.

As a Black woman working in a higher education institution steeped in status quo, I am aware that calling out institutional powers in demand for justice is risky. Institutions have engaged in the suppression of Black voices for times untold. Our lack of representation on tables, spaces, and positions of power is not new. In fact, the current institutional practice of performative visualization of representation is another manifestation of this injustice. This is where, as a Black woman at these institutions, I often have to choose between using my superpowers for liberatory work or acquiescing to the status quo. "Black women in America are morally bound to be justice seeking whole human beings. Even in the face of being told, sometimes relentlessly so, that we are less than whole, we are less than human" (Townes, 2014, 10:33). Choosing to seek justice within these institutions, although warned by an older Black female colleague to never put in writing what I would not want to see displayed on a headline, I continue to write. It serves notice, it creates a record, and the responses, or lack thereof, provide receipts. I choose writing because it is a powerful liberatory tool. Within the institution, I have used writing to fight racism and patriarchy, and I choose to view the risk involved as the price to be paid for meaningful liberatory work to take place.

When the Black Lives Matter movement attempted to reawaken global consciousness around racism in the summer of 2020, besides emails from college leaders condemning violence, many liberal institutions believed that their progressive research exempted them from addressing the need for structural change in their own institutions. But that historical moment required institutions that perpetuate oppression on minoritized people to take deeper looks within for the reexamination of their own inequities (Ellis, 2020). With more than 20 years of labor in institutions where the preservation of White comfort is predominant and normalized, and where male dominance often goes unchallenged, I have had to drink warrior fuel and stand under unwanted spotlights for the sake of justice.

After being asked to present before a group of college administrators on the use of a newly implemented digital platform to track students' academic performance, a high-ranking college official publicly berated me. After the meeting he placed an arm around my shoulders and whispered that he had been pressured to respond because one of my slides contained students' names and could be interpreted as a breach of privacy. His behavior, while condescending and paternalistic, was highly misogynistic. In a letter to Human Resources about his behavior, which I requested to be placed on his file, I wrote the following:

> The choice of words, gestures, and tone, all these communication indicators came across as a public reprimand for breaching protocol. The incident also highlighted very troubling aspects of a continuing power dynamic in academic circles—that a White male in one of the highest positions of power on the campus would feel justified to publicly raise his voice to rebuke a professional presentation by a woman of African descent. . . . In this day and age, and in any other arena, this unseemly display would evoke censure. Academia should not be the exception. (N. Blackman-Richards, personal communication, December 5, 2019)

In a public letter drafted and cosigned along with four other colleagues, all women of color, to the college administration, we challenged the institution for failing to appropriately address a hate crime. We posit that in their subtle dismissal of the crime, they inflicted psychological harm upon an entire community of employees of color:

> Faculty and Staff members have expressed sentiments of deep uncertainty about their safety. Many detailed feeling, "unsettled and violated" as well as "unsupported and ignored by the . . . administration." Aside from these feelings of overwhelm and fears of being alone in . . . going forward, many noted that this most recent incident has left them convinced that there are no safe spaces for BIPOC people on campus. [X building] was believed to be a sacred place of communing, learning, gathering, and healing. The blatant violation of this in the form of white supremacist messaging has left building occupants feeling unsafe and unprotected. Many fear not being able to offer students a safe space from the racially motivated microaggressions and "macroaggressions" they often face on our campus and in their classrooms. At this time, we ask for more than words. We have experienced implementation from a solely administrative level as ineffective, as it is often unaware of its continued upholding of a systematically biased status quo.
>
> Therefore, we respectfully request a time-sensitive action plan that will restore the confidence and faith of students, faculty and staff who have been deeply affected by this most recent incident in their own "home." (N. Blackman-Richards et al., public email, January 11, 2022)

In a letter to campus Public Safety leadership for promoting racial stereotypes and dismissing incidents connected to the above hate crime, including a threat to a Black female faculty member, I wrote the following:

> Instead dismissing and gaslighting communications, minimizing community concerns, labeling of justified fears, and ensuing trauma, micro-invalidating of our history and experiences, overlooking the health and safety of employees, along with trite divide and conquer tactics have been the tools of choice. As members of long-standing [campus] communities, we are experiencing these tools as the continuous infliction of harm.
>
> There is emotional and psychological damage that the mishandling of this incident has unleashed on an entire community. This damage has had significant consequences. . . . There is still work to be done to center the humanity of the [building] occupants. . . . There is a continued "stubborn resolve," to put it mildly, to disconnect the hate crime found on the board on January 6th with the threat to Dr. X's life, and to larger incidents like the bomb threats on HBCU's and recently X College in New York. The latest and only communication this year to the campus community about an "African American Man, wearing a black coat and blue hat"—a vague racialized description that only feeds into stereotypes—marks an extremely troubling pattern of continued racialized dismissiveness by Public Safety leadership. (N. Blackman-Richards, personal communication, March 25, 2022)

These self-defining and self-determining moments were high-risk decisions that came with personal and professional repercussions. While I labor for an institution that has outlined labor policies against employer retaliation, the shadowy presence of sidelining, scrutiny, and backroom undermining still came through. In the case of the hate crime, our requests for safety were eventually met, but these events also taught me valuable lessons about how we manifest our African Warrior Queenship and how we need to refuel to protect its glory. We must practice self-definition to protect our true selves. "If I didn't define myself for myself, I would be crunched into other people's fantasies for me and eaten alive" (Lorde, 1982, speech).

We manifest our African Queen Warrior powers in liberatory work that often challenges institutional powers and structures. Freedom is embedded in our ancestral DNA, so we must seek it by any means necessary. But we must also realize that liberatory work within our current racist, sexist, and classist structures is exhausting. Many of us have been spiritually depleted and have suffered physical and mental breakdowns in the process of carrying out this work. We often feel caught between remaining silent or taking a stand; but even silence takes its toll. Refueling is critical if we are to keep sane and thrive.

REFUELING: PROTECTING OUR AFRICAN WARRIOR QUEENSHIP

Racial battle fatigue is the exhaustion that people of color experience from repeated exposure to racism and the negative impact on their emotional, physiological, and psychological health and well-being (Quaye et al., 2019). The persistent emotional management of White people's feelings (What will they think? Say? How will they react?), along with not being able to express the full range of our emotions, can exacerbate racial battle fatigue (Evans & Moore, 2015). Given the emotional and mental investment required to do the work in spaces, places, and during moments that have been systematically unyielding, we need to find our own tools for survival and use them to refuel our energies. Refueling will allow us to be present to continue and sustain the work *and* ourselves. Echavarria and Williams (2022) recommend that we

> heed the signs of pain that we experience in our bodies from reaching capacity, the mental and emotional strain which comes with holding our own racial trauma . . . the everyday wear and tear of being Black and women, and the impact this has on the different roles and responsibilities in all dimensions of our lives. (p. 157)

To refuel is a mandate to deter getting stuck in the idea that our lives rotate around the pleasure of the status quo, it is living a lie.

Jacqueline Grant (2014) warns us,

> Don't live our lives in a lie. We cannot live our lives in the folds of old wounds. It's not healthy. It's not life giving. It doesn't bring in justice. It doesn't bring in the next generation. . . . Take seriously that this is land of the free. Create spaces and more spaces of freedom. (10:54)

The first space for freedom that we must create is the one for ourselves. An individual space that allows us to refuel and protect our African Warrior Queenship by preserving, replenishing, coalescing, and loving. The nature of the following four liberatory practices is intended to serve as salve to be placed on battle wounds from the wars that we often fight.

Self-Preserve

The concept of self-care has been co-opted to mean self-pampering, while centering a drive toward consumerism. The truth is that taking intentional efforts to self-care is self-preservation. We cannot fight every battle, so we must choose which ones we will invest our energies in. We must also come away from the battlefield, lay down our arms, and rest (*English Standard Version Bible*, 2001, Matt 11:28). For some, preserving energies may mean learning to say no, and not feeling that we need to sit at every table. While Audre Lorde (1988) was dying of cancer from overextending herself fighting oppressive systems, she famously wrote, "Caring for myself is not self-indulgence, it is self-preservation, and that is an act of political warfare" (p. 130). By Lorde's definition, self-care is an act of resistance and defiance. In a 1993 study, McEwen and Stellar pointed out that high allostatic loads or allostatic overload occurs when bad stress happens too frequently and chronically and, as a result, a person develops so much wear and tear on the body and brain from being in a chronically heightened stress state that the body reacts poorly to the stress and begins to break itself down. Some 14 years later, another study discovered that Black women have higher allostatic loads in comparison to White women, White men, and Black males, irrespective of socioeconomic status (Tan et al., 2017). Finding ways to temporarily disconnect while you recover is an important part of self-preservation. In their study of racial battle fatigue, Quaye et al. (2019) found that "disconnecting, or unplugging" (p. 111), as an approach to self-care was one that participants described as enabling them to remove themselves physically, emotionally, and mentally from the racial battle fatigue they were experiencing. Prioritizing our self-preservation means giving ourselves permission to turn the phone off, step away from the computer, and prioritize self-care.

Replenish

Replenishing is finding moments and ways to cleanse the heart and mind to refresh them from the burdens of the struggles we endure and the battles we must wage. As Black women leaders we need to find ways of replenishing from all the racism, oppression, sexism, stress, and toxicity that could ravish our hearts and minds. Echavarria and Williams (2022) recommend "Taking a break, having moments of stillness, reflecting on our thoughts and feelings, examining bodily sensations, and remembering what brings us joy, are practices which promote our well-being" (p. 157). It is in the intentional seeking of replenishment that we tap into our creative spirits. The arts have replenishing power—drawing, painting, dancing, and so forth. We must find daily moments of joy as well as time to breathe and self-affirm. Joy will shift our focus and balance our energies. Breathing will allow us to center our focus on the present. Self-affirmations will force us to rewrite any negative narratives or messaging that could distract us from our purpose.

Coalesce

Time and time again, Black women have proven that there is power in coalition. Smith (2022) assures us that seeking out an accountability partner who is a Black women leader to support you with your self-care plan or creating a radical self-care group for Black women focused on helping one another to create and maintain healthy self-care pathways is critical. Black women must also coalesce under the understanding that with all our educational achievements, professional accolades, and buying power, we are not yet free. Shirley Chisholm's (1971) call is still applicable today: "Women in this country must become revolutionaries. We must refuse to accept the old—the traditional roles and stereotypes" (p. 21). Our coalitions must arm us with strategic wisdom as well as community care responsibilities, for we must look out for each other's well-being. In the same article Chisholm ends by stating that the task will not be easy, but the power for social change "lies in our hands . . . we must use our power well and we must use it wisely" (p. 21).

Love

The most radical form of resistance we can release upon this world is love. Love for ourselves. Love for our families. Love for our community. Love for our people. We are reminded by bell hooks (1994) in her essay "Love Is the Practice of Freedom" that love is the greatest form of resistance: "The moment we choose to love we begin to move against dominations, against oppression" (p. 250). She goes on to encourage a love ethic that focuses on the importance of service to others. We need to be guided by the principle that as African Warrior Queens, we resist because we love ourselves and our people enough to want to fight for the survival of that love. Poet Porsha Olayiwola (2022) describes Black love:

> It is political, it is revolutionary. To be a Black person and to love a Black person in a world that wants to kill Black people, in a world that tells Black people that they are ugly that they are invaluable, that they are unintelligent, is a testament to just living and surviving. (35:25)

While this world continues to operate within imposed legacies of sexism and racism, Black women leaders will continue to be misunderstood, undervalued, and undermined. They will undoubtedly face injustices. The ability to stand on the examples of their ancestors and the women who paved the way before them and glean from their strategic wisdom will provide the fuel needed to persist. By arming themselves through re-memorializing and refueling for liberatory work, Black women must appeal to their superpowers. The realization that our intersections are our superpowers will allow us to stand in the strength of our African Warrior Queenship. In one of several moving scenes in *The Woman King*, King Ghezo, after realizing that Nanisca disobeyed him and went to rescue the Agojie that had been captured, responds to her request to resign her command by giving a rousing speech to his people. One of Ghezo's statements embodies the manifestation of our superpowers: "There is power in our minds, our culture, our unity. We are limitless if we understand our power" (Stevens, 2016). For her bravery, the king elevates Nanisca and she becomes "The Woman King." Though often unacknowledged, the insight of Black women and their ability to lead from that insight is powerful. Black women have proven this time and again. Yet, as they continue to use their superpowers to challenge systems, structures, and institutions, it is imperative that Black women become intentional to refuel in order to sustain themselves, the work, and the generation of women who will follow their examples.

Part II

A WOMAN WILL MANIFEST

Whitneé Garrett-Walker

When Black women speak, God, our Ancestors, and the Earth listens. Our prayers, tears, moans, songs, and rhythms are sometimes the only way we can get our breakthroughs. "A Woman Will Manifest" is the tale we lived to tell. Telling our stories of redemption is the fruit of our manifestation because we're still here. We're grounded with roots as deep and lush as the many oak and magnolia trees stained with our blood. We reclaim these trees as Kin because they didn't consent to our pain, just as we did not consent to our own. Their existence is an ontological manifestation of our right to do more than exist. Black women are the biggest upset to the systems and structures of oppression that seek to drown us. Our existence and our commitment to leadership remain an example of how we continue to manifest the future, past, and present. To this end, this section was written with the spirit of refusal where the challenges and troubles of leadership are defined, deconstructed, and remade into stepping stones. The counter-narratives in this section speak to the many ways that Black women *make a way out of no way*, but not without telling how they crossed the bridge over troubled water. As you read, we invite you to tap into your own stories of triumph and redemption to remind yourself of why you're even here, leading, to begin with.

Chapter 5

Life, Love, and Leadership

Rachelle Rogers-Ard

She came after me. Relentlessly pursuing my excellence, the need for "someone like you." Over and over articulating the need for what I bring, for my lens, for my brilliance. Lunches instead of traditional interview sessions; meetings over breakfast as part of the mating ritual. She put an engagement ring on it through a low-risk consultative relationship used to gauge my work product. Together, we created vows designed to show my value; this new relationship would reinforce her commitment to embedding me and my work into the leadership structure. We formally married in September. By May the next year, after the George Floyd murder, I knew divorce was imminent.

I have been researching, observing, and writing about Black female leaders for the past 15 years. From Jones and Shorter-Gooden (2003), Bell and Nkomo (2001), and Thompkins (2005) to Mullen and Robertson (2014), Rogers-Ard (2016), and Rogers-Ard and Knaus (2020), my intellectual knowledge and awareness of the ways in which Black women are expected to work twice as hard for half the financial and institutional acknowledgment has been well-documented. The recent emotional and ideological lynching of Judge Ketanji Brown Jackson, as demonstrated by the many confrontational and contentious interview questions steeped in intersectionally racist beliefs (Hulse, 2022), is yet another example of the ways in which Black women are consistently demeaned, devalued, and degraded publicly at the hands of men and women who are clearly far inferior—yet Black women are asked to show little to no emotional response. Black women's stoicism alternately reinforces myths about their inability to feel pain while also providing society with ideological whips designed to continually break a woman's spirit. As one Black female colleague shared, "It's the constant disrespect that wears me out!" (personal communication, 2022).

This chapter outlines a specific time in my leadership journey that shifted my entire perspective and changed my life. I write from the nuanced perspective as a Black woman and share my experience on a systemic educational plantation where the emotional pain and disrespect came through hands similar in color to mine. As a qualitative narrative researcher, I use stories to inform my own firsthand experiences. While researchers have been using narrative analysis for years (Andrews et al., 2004; Chase, 2003; Fraser, 2004; Riessman, 1993; Sandelowski, 1991; Schlein, 2020), my work creates the ability to understand, draw from, and affirm Afrocentric ways of knowing by centering my voice. In Afrocentrism, knowing is rooted in nature, ancestral wisdom, and community; often those knowings are passed from person to person through story (Kaya, 2014; Ngara, 2007). Further, "Indigenous and Afrocentric epistemologies offer powerful worldviews, a term used to describe the collective thought process of a people or culture" (Safir & Dugan, 2021, p. 17).

I use a narrative approach grounded in Afrocentric storytelling to share my experiences, highlight learning jewels, validate, and ease the burden of other Black women who aspire to the Majestic Place, as described in the introduction to this text. My reflections are italicized and separated by spaces with analysis following each narrative. As a Black cisgender female over 50, I am using my story and experiential learning to derive meaning, to provide a cautionary tale for other Black women, and as a means of accountability for folx who work with, and try to manage, Black women. In this way, I lean heavily on Dillard's (2021) notion of the endarkened feminist epistemology (EFE): This embodied a distinguishable difference in cultural standpoint based in our intersectional socializations of race, gender, and other identities and the historical and contemporary context of oppressions and resistance for African-American women, including the oppressions and dismissal of our spiritual knowing as theoretical and epistemological tools for us to think with (p. 15).

In addition to using narrative methodology, I have chosen to place this story in the format of a relationship, because all interactions with humans are relationships. We are created for connection and belonging (Brown, 2021; Cobb & Krownapple, 2019; Ginwright, 2022). I was off-kilter in this recent leadership role, not unlike the ways in which I have been off-kilter in many of my romantic relationships. Over time, my reflection has allowed me to see this experience as part of the Black woman's struggle around life, love, and leadership. This experience was rooted in intersectional and internalized racism; I learned concrete strategies to radically love myself, and this journey was centered on female leadership.

While I understand proximity to whiteness within our country's caste system (Wilkerson, 2020), I believe I was less vigilant in this new position, even going so far as to relax my head's swivel (symbolized by the way in which Black people consistently look out for attacks by moving our heads in a circular motion) that I had previously normalized working in traditional, White-led organizations designed to contain me. Because race and power are linked, I had to learn that some Black and non-Black leaders of color replicate White-framed systems to hoard power and silence Black women. Key to this story is the understanding that "all skin folk ain't kinfolk"; this is not the usual tale of the Black/White binary so often discussed (Armour, 2020; Bell & Nkomo, 2001; Muhammad, 2019). Instead, I wanted to share the ways in which my experiences with Black women and women of color have been, in many ways, even more deleterious in my journey. I have been prepared since birth to deal with White people, white supremacy culture, and White women trying to manage me the way they have since slavery; that is my norm, my way of understanding workplaces, and my burden to bear while accessing educational and professional spaces. However, my experience at the hands of Black and Brown women who replicated white supremacist systems was hard to manage, difficult to understand, and somewhat surprising. Let's begin.

DATING

I knew who she was. Most local folks in my field knew of her and had heard of her work; being born and raised in Ashtown meant that most everyone knew everybody. We went to the same university several years apart. I met her twice—once when we attended an alumni function and another time when we were both asked to serve on a committee for our alma mater. She was always beautifully dressed, regal with just enough hipness to be accessible. I thought she was a beautiful, queenly, Black woman, and I really respected and liked her.

Later, she ran for public office and hosted a fundraiser. My young son attended, and one of his schoolteachers mentioned that The One wanted to speak to me. He came home and, of course, did not get anything right about that exchange. "Ms. Hutter told me some lady wanted to talk to you," and that was as far as it got.

A couple of months later, I found out Ms. Hutter passed on my information when The One contacted me via email: "Would love to talk to you about your work; let me know a good time" was basically the message, but I am embarrassed at how excited I was that she reached out—to ME! I immediately responded and waited to hear. It was a while, but a meeting was finally scheduled.

Understanding how fashionable this Black woman was and knowing that I couldn't just show up at the office looking any old type of way meant a week of finding just the right outfit. The heels were no problem, but the fit had to say,

"What? This old thing I just jumped into this morning without any thought and am totally coordinated down to my toenails? With a bag to die for?"

I finally got myself together and attended the meeting. When I arrived, I was surprised to see another person waiting as well. I marched to the receptionist and said, "Dr. Rachelle Rogers-Ard to see The One." The White male, clearly listening, said, "Oh, you're here as well?" Before I could answer, we were both shown into the inner sanctum.

We had a productive meeting discussing possibilities to support building out the kind of program in which The One was interested. After the meeting, the White male asked, "Do you want to get together to work on a proposal?" I was sure I did not; this was my opportunity to show my brilliance, and I couldn't take the chance that it would be usurped by a colonizer. I simply indicated I would respond via email and went directly home to work on . . . sending in a proposal. I made the Black woman connection by sending the email directly to The One. She responded that they would be in touch, and I didn't hear anything for about six months. I thought that was it.

Six months later, The One contacted me via text asking to meet in Ashtown, away from the office. I took that as a good sign. We had three of those meetings at various coffee shops and restaurants around town, talking about the work but also getting to know each other. I didn't understand it at the time, but those were informal interviews.

The One and I decided I should be a consultant for the company. I was excited (way too much, actually) to have an opportunity to not only do work that would be rewarding but also to work with this dope, Christian, Black woman.

Understanding Black women's leadership is about "(re)cognizing we already know. We already have within us a righteous and just knowing" (Dillard, 2021, p. 87). I now realize I had been seeking a Black female mentor—someone from whom I could learn, but also someone who would be a model for the type of leadership I knew was different with Black women. I received wonderful Black female leadership when I was a novice teacher. My principal, in addition to having a dope hairstyle and fashion sense to match, took the time to mold me and ensure that I was poised for success. Later, that same principal "voluntold" me to work with another Black female leader who—again!—molded and nurtured me, supplying extensive training, and became a surrogate mother figure to help me develop my craft. Those two Black women were instrumental in my becoming more than a teacher; they showed me how to be an educator.

I was actively seeking a Black female leader who would reaffirm my belief in the special sauce that is Black female leadership. Brené Brown (2018) says, "Who you are is how you lead" (p. 11). With love and respect, I elevate to who you are, and your racial context is how you lead. I cannot separate race from who I am, and my three core values of faith, family, and integrity greatly influence the way I lead. Direct reports have indicated that I am proud of my faith; I create a familial-like organizational culture, and I honor trust. I am an effective leader because I treat people well by being equally interested and invested in their development. This leadership stance is based on the way the two Black women discussed above have poured into my life over time, and I honor them with my leadership.

Those same two Black women helped me understand that Black women and fashion are intricately linked. As I have gotten older, I realize that Black women dress for us first, then for men. As evidenced by Amanda Seales's comedic routine, Black women compliment each other by naming what we see: "OK, polka dots!" (ariemasuccess, LLC, 2022). As a result, I remember vividly being aware of the way I would need to dress, including accessories, if I was to fit into a space with a Black female leader. Having been raised by a single Black mother and being a member of a traditionally Black church for more than 30 years, my lived experience is that Black women see fashion as more than just clothing and shoes; we understand that our attire reflects the way we will be viewed by others. Many Black female leaders are hyper-aware of their appearance, using fashion as both armor and advertisement to set the tone for their leadership.

More than wanting and needing a Black female role model, I had experienced challenges in previous roles reporting to White women (Rogers-Ard, 2016) who needed to feel relevant, needed to micromanage, or wanted to develop a false friendship to prove they were "woke." The two times I reported to White men, I found myself managing up in a way that felt natural and familiar. I wanted a Black female leader who would shift all those negative experiences into positive, high-five-giving, chuckles-behind-the-hand, knowing looks across the room workplace.

THE PROPOSAL

I began consulting with the company for a year. Given The One's schedule, it was difficult to move the work forward with haste, but we began slowly planning and looking for ways to implement the project. My consulting contract was extended in the second year because of a small planning grant. At one of the planning sessions, The One said, "You know, you might as well come to work for us full-time." I honestly didn't think she was serious; I said something like "I plan to die at my company," and she let it go—for a while. Soon, however, she began talking about what it could look like to bring me on full-time and we began having those conversations in earnest. I was asked to send my ideas to help craft a job description which seemed like a positive sign, even though I was still undecided.

ENGAGEMENT

I knew things were getting serious when The One had me meet with her #2 for lunch. By this time I was savvy enough to understand that this was an informal interview. #2 and I met and then I was called into meetings to discuss ways to help our satellite offices, proposed bodies of work, and salary. I knew I was in when The One invited me to her home with other company leaders for a brainstorming session! I felt seen, heard, and valued to be part of the inner leadership circle before even having a formal contract. I vividly remember The One asking for my opinion and expertise. These were her senior officers in the room, yet my input was valued. I was ready to be a part of this organization.

Over the next few months, The One and #2 began the process of creating a position for me. They included me on the job description drafting. We discussed ways in which I could bring value and fill gaps in the organization, and brainstormed ideas about taking over bodies of work that had been dormant with other employees. I began to get excited about this new position—but I didn't have it yet.

To ensure we followed protocol, I had to apply and complete two interviews for the role. I prepared for those interviews as if I was defending my dissertation; I wanted to demonstrate both my proficiency for the work as well as ensure I didn't let The One down. During that process, I learned that I would be the only Black person at that level of the organization; there were other women of color, but I would be the only Black person at that level. The information did not bother me at that time; later, I would understand the significance.

It feels good to be wanted. The ways in which white supremacy culture exists in professional spaces has underscored my reality that as a Black woman it is never good enough to be good enough; I must always be better than. I have lived my adult professional life understanding that part of my Black female tax is consistently proving and justifying my brilliance for others. But when a Black female senior leader recognizes and values my contributions, it feels good. So good, in fact, that I overlooked potential red flags.

I was excited that the senior leader of this organization wanted to talk with me about my work and was doubly excited to begin the process of consulting. It took me much longer than it should have to understand that I was basically auditioning for a more permanent future role. Then, when a role was created within the organization, I felt victorious; surely this was what all the years of demanding work was leading toward. In my mind, the opportunity to work with female leaders of color who appreciated, valued, and respected my contributions was the apex of my professional career. My longing for a Black female role model and my trauma from existing within white supremacy organizational culture left me wide open to future possibilities. I noticed and accepted that I would be the only Black woman at my level within the organization; I thought of it as a data point but not a huge red flag. I noticed there were other women of color at the senior level and dismissed wondering why the Black female leader of the organization would not create opportunities for other Black female leaders.

MARRIAGE

The One made me an official job offer in June 2019 and put a ring on it! I had taken part in company retreats, attended small meetings with leaders, and was ready to jump in. I decided to take an extended vacation as I left my other job; I didn't want anything to hinder what I was sure would be my next long-term position. Prior to starting, I was asked to facilitate a retreat for one of the business units; I was overly prepared because this would be a prelude to my actual employment. I received excellent feedback, and in September 2019 I arrived at my new place of employment ready to go!

First Harbinger of Trouble

My position was close to the top of the organizational chart. There were people at my position, then chiefs, then The One. It is critical to note that I accepted the position mid-June but did not begin until September, so imagine my surprise when I arrived at the building but had no office ready. I was told they were moving several business units and was shown to a lovely but incomplete cubicle. I hadn't been in a cubicle in more than 10 years! #2, to whom I now had a dual reporting relationship, asked sweetly but insincerely, "I hope this is OK?" It wasn't. It really wasn't, but to demonstrate being a team player, I responded, "I can work anywhere." The cubicle had no chair and no plastic mat to place on the carpet so a chair could roll; I wasn't told my phone number, and I had no supplies.

The cubicle was in a department where another person at my level had a large office within eyesight. I already knew her, and she showed me where her department kept supplies. I was able to get some pens, folders, and other items, resolving of course, like many Black women, to "make do." I went into the hallway and found a chair; I asked around to see if there was an extra plastic mat available and found one on the first floor and dragged it up to my cubicle.

I ordered what I needed from Amazon. A few kind folks helped me learn about my phone and find out my actual extension, and the head of IT was extremely helpful with my laptop and getting me adjusted. All on the first day in heels.

A couple of weeks later, I saw two of my former students of color who now worked at this company. They immediately pulled me aside, shoved me into the elevator, and took me down to the basement level. They told me this was where they could talk if they didn't want people to know. I asked them about talking outside, but they told me employees would look out the window then ask them what they were talking about when they went back inside. This seemed ominous.

Many Black women are, by nature and as a response to racism, extremely resilient, with a "can do, make do" attitude that I have always relied upon and loved. The notion of not having an office ready on my first day was out of line. Looking back, I believe that my silence was about two things: (1) I didn't want to rock the boat on my very first day and come off looking like a diva; and (2) I was happy with the position, the salary, the work to come, and wanted to make a good impression. Also, I did not want to embarrass The One, given the fact that she created a brand-new position for me for which she had fought on a political level. I now realize this was a test orchestrated by #2. As mentioned above, Black women are consistently faced with having to prove their worth and being assessed daily. This test was to see how I responded to being placed in a cubicle directly across from another woman with the same title whose office was huge. What we know about white supremacy culture is that space is equal to power and certainly holds meaning within corporate organizations. I did not realize all of this in the moment, but I now see that publicly placing the only Black person at that level in the organization in a cubicle was a way of knocking me down to size like White folks, non-Black folx of color, and some Black folx with internalized racist beliefs have been doing to "uppity" Black folx since slavery.

However, not unlike the way in which Black people have been helping one another to survive since slavery, a few folx of color reached out to support me right away. Those basement meetings became "hush harbors" (Dillard, 2021): frequent and secret respites from the overbearing and soul-sucking white supremacy culture. As folx of color, we were literally replicating historic meetings where upstairs represented oppression and downstairs represented freedom. As time went on, I used the basement meetings to vent, strategize, and find support from a few Black employees and one person of color who took time to help me think through oppressive situations. I am thankful for those employees today and reminded that Black folx need affinity spaces to counteract daily intersectionally racist encounters. It is also interesting to note that while the organization was demographically diverse, white supremacy culture (Okun & Jones, 2000) elements of fear, perfectionism, and defensiveness were perpetuated by many non-Black women of color within the organization.

Second Harbinger of Trouble

One of my "hush harbor" sistas offered me the use of her office, given that her work was mainly in the field. When I told #2 about the offer, she was reluctant (who would be able to watch me if I was in an office with a closed door?), but my colleague and former student had already gotten approval from her senior manager, and it would have looked petty for #2 to refuse. I moved into my colleague's office gratefully and thankfully. The box of candy I gave her was woefully inadequate.

Weeks later, I went to the bathroom during a meeting #2 and I were attending with other employees. Shortly thereafter, I received a text message from #2:

"Where are you?"
"In the bathroom"
"Still?"

I didn't answer. I am clearly a grown woman. I've been going to bathrooms on my own without needing anyone to ask me questions for decades.

After receiving no answer, #2 texted: "Well, hurry up; I don't want anyone to ask where you are."

I took my time returning from the bathroom. I went to the ground floor for water and waited to fill my canister with ice from the dispenser. I took the stairs to my office and then sauntered back to the meeting, where I found I hadn't missed much. #2 looked at me as if she wanted to rebuke me for my actions, but I ignored her and suddenly became immersed in taking notes. I accepted marriage to The One but was tied to #2 like an in-law ... and was growing weary.

Black people being constantly watched derives from slavery. Light-skinned and mixed-race female slaves were allowed into the Big House; those who were of darker tones had to work in the fields. The dehumanization of Black people meant that Africans enslaved in the US territories had to work from sunup to sundown, with little rest and extraordinarily little food (Kendi, 2016). Slaveholders hired Whites who had fewer resources to become overseers to watch Africans. Because there was always a fear that enslaved Africans would escape, Whites remained vigilant in watching and punishing enslaved Africans, both as a reminder that they were in charge and as a notice for other Africans (Baptist, 2016).

This notion of constantly being watched that began during the US chattel slavery system as a means of anti-Blackness continued through the Jim Crow era, through and during the US civil rights movement of the 1960s and 1970s and is still prevalent today. Collins (1998) discusses the politics of containment wherein Black women are used for their visibility of diversity and perceived inclusion while simultaneously masking the invisibility of racist policies designed to keep them in their place. It is Muhammad's (2019) condemnation of Blackness that predisposes White people to think of Black folx as inherently criminal, as demonstrated most recently with "Karens," White men, and other non-Black people calling the police on Black people doing everyday tasks and extends to the assassination of Trayvon Martin, Jayland Walker, and countless others.

As Wilkerson (2020) notes:

> Modern-day caste protocols are less often about overt attacks or conscious hostility and can be dispiritingly hard to fight. They are like the wind, powerful enough to knock you down but invisible as they go about their work. They are sustained by the muscle memory of relative rank and the expectation of how one interacts with others based on their place in the hierarchy. It's a form of status hyper-vigilance, the entitlement of the dominant caste to step in and assert itself wherever it chooses, to monitor or dismiss those deemed beneath them as they see fit. (p. 212)

For Black women working in White supremacist systems, the notion of watching becomes even more prevalent under the guise of monitoring effectiveness and productivity. In the situation above, I was being watched and policed for going to the bathroom and contacted to learn how long I would be out of the meeting. I still wonder why I bothered to respond to the text at all. I am convinced this non-Black woman of color would never have sent a text to a White man inquiring about his bathroom habits. Her anti-Black need to surveil me became clear with her text.

Also, the ploy of using the ubiquitous "us" to manipulate people into subservience does not work on me and never has. Brené Brown (2018) calls this the "Invisible Army," where armored leaders try to provide a sense of community purpose when chastising or wanting Black women to do something they feel is lacking. As a result, Black women are statistically among the most likely to need time off but not take it, even when our own health is at stake (Chinn et al., 2021). Even when other colleagues have an easier lift, most Black women readily take on additional tasks because we know it is usually easier for us to do it ourselves rather than waiting for someone else, and we understand that our productivity is often called into question. This sense of having to do more, be more, show more, demonstrate more is not sustainable and can only be disrupted when Black women understand the linkage to slavery and sharecropping. By convincing ourselves that we must perform for White and non-Black folx of color, we remain on a hustle carousel where we are only as good as our last success. In this way, we replicate slavery's legacy of trying to be the person who has picked the largest bale of cotton.

Third Harbinger of Trouble

I received a call from a senior leader at my previous organization requesting that I facilitate a series of retreats for his staff. I immediately told #2, who told me that I needed to focus on my new role. When I pushed back, indicating that part of my role was to support local organizations, she said, "Did you hear me? I said NO!" I left her office and immediately called my mom. "I'm about to go smooth off, and it's only my second month." Mom told me to calm down and pray. After I did that, I decided I needed to speak to #2. I asked if I could provide some feedback and let her know that speaking to me like that was out of line. She seemed to take it well, telling me that she appreciated my feedback, and that we were in the "get to know each other" phase of our relationship. But I knew something was off.

When I told the senior leader from my previous organization that #2 had said no, he reached out to The One, who met with me, without #2, and said she was inclined to let me help support the leader—on a limited basis—and would let #2 know. While #2 never said anything else to me, I know that did not sit well with her. What I should have known was her personality was not one where she could let something like that go.

One of the continuous sticking points between me and #2 was my relationship with The One; it became increasingly clear that #2 did not want her direct reports talking with The One at any time. One day, I walked into a meeting with #2 wearing jeans. Now, let's be clear, when I wear jeans to work, I'm also wearing a heel, nice blouse, jacket, pearls, jewelry, and matching bag. #2 said,

"You know you can't wear jeans at this level."

I said, "I'm pretty sure I've seen people wearing jeans."

"Well, at this level; we can't wear jeans, and The One doesn't allow them."

I paused for a moment and said, "Is this in the HR manual?"

"No, it's not, but The One doesn't like jeans, and at this level we have to set the standard."

At this point, I was tired of #2, so I went to the HR manager and asked if there was anything in writing about not wearing jeans. There was not. So I asked The One,

"Hey, I heard I can't wear jeans; is that true?"

The One said, "I've seen #2 wearing her jeans. I may have mentioned something to her, but you can wear jeans, just not to formal meetings."

So I had my answer, and I was fine with it.

Two days later, #2 found her way to my office (where she never previously visited) wearing—you guessed it—jeans. She came in, sat down, and proceeded to hold a meaningless conversation. Because I could see her just waiting for me to have a reaction of any kind, I totally ignored her jeans, completed the conversation, and moved on.

While I was trying to balance these varying differences, I was also meeting with The One outside of work to manage a couple of other projects. I became aware this was a problem when #2 said to me, "You should know that everything you say to The One will get back to me; she and I meet frequently and don't have any secrets." I had no idea why she needed to tell me that, but I knew that was her issue and not mine.

Our strengths and weaknesses are on full display as leaders; we show a deeper level of who we are when we are placed in positions of leadership. Leaders must manage other adults, create opportunities for adults to be productive, and are held to exacting standards for completing huge bodies of work. Executive leaders, like #2, have added pressures when leading huge organizational divisions. While leading a team can be difficult, the job of leading several teams within a division is fraught with pitfalls and requires an extremely confident and highly productive person to be in that role. However, many people have unresolved self-doubt that surfaces when we are leading groups of people. Moving in a White supremacist organizational culture based largely on patriarchy creates another layer of difficulty; female leaders must grapple with being seen as strong but not traditionally masculine; being effective but also nurturing. Fighting against these cisgender stereotypes affects all female leaders. Then, when women of color are placed in leadership roles, intersectional (Crenshaw, 2013) racism plays a huge part in making these roles even more difficult.

While I understand women of color and their complex leadership roles, it is also true that many women of color manage to be phenomenal leaders despite these circumstances. When analyzing those who do not lead well, like #2, actions reveal character. #2's desire to belittle me by placing me in a cubicle instead of an office like all the other people in the organization at my level, her continuous watching of me rooted in anti-Blackness, and her disrespect by treating me like a child through her response to my previous organization's request were rooted in her own insecurities about her leadership. To be clear, I am not making excuses for #2's behavior; rather, I seek to understand it in hopes that should I be faced with that kind of character in the future, I will be able to draw on this experience to help navigate the situation.

Had I not received permission to work with my previous organization, my relationship with #2 might have remained at passive aggression; however, the permission that effectively overturned her decision was seen as a betrayal—not from me, but from The One. This is what led to #2 reminding me that she and The One had a great relationship devoid of secrets. Leaders who need to remind people that they are, indeed, the leader show their own lack of leadership ability by consistently undermining and trying to control those who display confidence. The issue around #2's relationship with The One was again indicative of her own lack of confidence. Perhaps she was concerned that because both The One and I were Black women, she would somehow be left out, or perhaps she had experienced someone coming between her and The One and didn't want that to happen again. Whatever the reason, her leadership was fraught with petty microaggressions and pushbacks designed to keep me off-kilter—some of which worked. Reporting to a senior female executive leader of color who sought to control me instead of leading me felt foreign, strange, and made me unsure. By the time of the jean incident, I knew I would not be in the marriage long-term.

Fourth Harbinger of Trouble

I created an anti-racist leadership development training series for all employees, ran it by #2, and sent out registration information. While I was away at a conference, #2 called and indicated that the Cabinet leaders decided to postpone the training. I already had 20 people registered, and many more had contacted me to indicate their interest. Apparently, Cabinet leaders were concerned about having people in the training without their permission. This would normally be fine, but the issue was that Cabinet leaders didn't want to tell their team members they couldn't take the training; they didn't want to be the bad guy. I was flabbergasted about the way in which our senior leaders wouldn't allow their employees to participate. It was decided that I would preview the learning for senior-level members first; then, upon approval, they would choose the employees who could participate. Given that The One was the only Black person on the Cabinet, I was concerned about this type of controlled dominance of a mostly-White senior leadership group. I was also concerned that The One didn't override Cabinet members and allow the session to move forward, given her previously voiced support for anti-racist work. I readily agreed to work with the Cabinet, but other concerns were more prevalent, and I never had an opportunity.

Later, in a meeting with #2, who was a non-Black woman of color, I named race as one issue within the organization. She asked, "Is everything about race for you?" to which I answered, "Yes!" I was tasked by The One to manage the organization's equity work with senior leaders but was met with pushback from leaders who felt like embedding race within equity work was a problem. I was slowly realizing that I wouldn't be able to do the type of meaningful work that I was called to do at this organization. I was still hopeful, and then George Floyd's murder happened. After my son challenged me to do more than attend demonstrations, I created an anti-racist curriculum that we could share with all our satellite offices. I immediately shared it with The One and #2, indicating that I would be willing to roll out a training series right away for our satellite leaders at no charge. The One said she was not "ready" to do that; #2 did not respond. In all fairness, we were also dealing with the beginning stages of the COVID-19 pandemic, but I couldn't understand how difficult it would be to take advantage of having people at home to offer a much-needed training around race, whiteness, and leadership. Once again, I realized that I wouldn't be able to do the work that was super-important to me at this organization, but I knew my work was greatly needed and timely.

As an example, our office receptionist was an older Black woman to whom I had spoken previously (in the way that Black women do: "Hey, there!" "How ya doin?" "Girl, I like those shoes!" "Just trying to be more like you!"), but I didn't really know her well. One day I saw a White man, younger than the receptionist, leaning over her desk deep in a one-sided conversation. I could tell she was uncomfortable but didn't want to interrupt the conversation. When I got a chance to walk by her desk again, the White man was gone, so I asked how she was. She seemed really dejected, so I asked if she was OK and if she needed anything. Slowly, she asked if she could share something with me.

Apparently, the White man, younger than she was and to whom she did not report, took the time to tell her about spelling errors in one of her emails. He let her know that she needed to work on it and shared "tips" about sending emails. Without her having to say anything more, I knew she was upset. When I asked if she had spoken to her supervisor about it, she said she didn't want to rock the boat. I asked how she wanted me to handle this information—I could either speak to the co-worker directly or could elevate to her manager without naming her. At first she told me to leave it alone, but later she told me it would be great if someone could handle the White male co-worker.

I shared this incident, without naming anyone, with senior leadership and let them know that this was the type of situation we could discuss in an anti-racist course. One of the senior leaders asked how I was made aware, and I told him, "People tell me things because they trust me; it's my Superpower." Later, The One met with me in her office and said that senior leadership was concerned about my Superpower. I didn't really understand. Wouldn't leaders want to know when their employees were being aggressed and hurt? Wouldn't leaders want to name issues that threatened organizational health?

The Black Lives Matter movement sparked a response from many organizations regarding race relations. Most organizations realized the need to have some type of response and created DEI task forces, race and equity positions, or developed book clubs to discuss race. I have always researched and discussed race, being critically aware of its impact on my identity and my positionality. When I work with Black people and non-Black people of color who are not interested in naming race, training their employees about race, and looking at ways to at least disrupt racist practices, I continue to push their thinking, understanding that fear is a huge barrier to race relations in this country.

Leaders of color in White-framed systems often don't want to be seen as "playing the race card" or naming race as a barrier to success. Here, the caste system (Wilkerson, 2020) comes into play in that many non-Black folx of color want to guard their status in the caste system by enacting anti-Black racism. My insistence that race is always a critical factor was surprising to the non-Black woman of color for whom race was seen as something tangential to her identity. I name race and racism because my Blackness is a crucial, critical part of my authentic being—not something I put on when the mood suits.

My naivete around my anti-racist curriculum came in the form of expecting a Black woman and non-Black woman of color to have the same goal as I: to work toward the disruption and dismantling of white supremacy. I was reminded that it isn't only White folx who hold up systems of supremacy; folx of color receive temporary privileges that they enjoy and guard jealously. My tunnel vision and assumption that we were all moving toward the same goal allowed me to be blind to the reality of this organization. My insistence on creating two training curricula without being asked could have been to my detriment. The senior leaders' decision to not allow their team members to participate and the pushback I received while having discussions about equity with senior leaders were all key performance indicators of the desire to maintain White-framed systems. I have since come to understand that, not unlike slaves who couldn't understand the need to escape, not everyone wants to be free. Fear is a powerful motivating factor, especially when facing the unknown.

My concern is for Black people, especially women, who remain in White-framed systems without an advocate to help make meaning of their situation. The unmitigated gall of a young White man telling an older Black woman to whom she did not report about spelling errors in her emails is one example of the ways in which the organization did not discuss intersectional racism. The organization could have benefited from deep DEI training to help understand how racial injustice manifests as intersectional microaggressions in the workplace (Moody & Lewis, 2019). Instead of being concerned about the oppression this Black woman faced, the senior leaders' fear of pulling back the covers, of peeling the onion to see the layers underneath, was larger than their ability to face the truth. Their anti-Black racism allowed a Black woman to suffer while allowing one White man to continue spreading his seed of patriarchal racism. My greatest regret during that time is that I was not able to help another Black sister.

DIVORCE

It was the early months of the pandemic, when people thought we would be back in our offices within three or four weeks. I was working on my anti-racist curriculum in hopes that we would be able to offer it to leaders across the region. I attended work meetings as scheduled, but during that time anything less than racial equity seemed meaningless to me.

I noticed a couple of things happening within the organization. First, #2 created a new team within her division and positioned a Latina as lead. I noticed the new team's subject area was in alignment with my work and asked The One if I could apply. There was no application process, and the other person was given the position. I also noticed that to create a team, #2 moved people from other teams to ensure the new team was fully staffed.

I still thought there was a chance to salvage this position, so when #2 came to me about a large state-funded grant for my work, I was happy to take on the challenge. #2 and I took meetings, landed outside partners, and I took the lead in pulling the grant together. I understood that leaders in this agency often brought in outside funding, but it was not a priority for my position, nor was it listed in my job description. We didn't get the grant, which made me ask The One if my position was in jeopardy. She indicated that the work was extremely important and that my position was already funded in next years' budget.

One day, during my 1:1, #2 asked if I had spoken with The One about my position. I told her I had and knew there was funding available. #2 then said, "I don't feel comfortable moving forward with this conversation because I think you should report to HR. Since the grant didn't come through, you really can't be at your level in the organization without having a team."

I must admit, I was blindsided.

Within the next few days, I had a meeting with The One, who indicated that because I didn't have a team, my work would be moved to HR. Of course that meant (1) losing my title, (2) decreasing my annual salary by more than $20K, and (3) losing my position. It was a demotion. I went over my employment contract with a fine-tooth comb; it did not mention needing a team to work at this level. I received this information the second week in June 2020. I told The One that I was uncomfortable with this treatment, and while I generally liked the head of HR, this was untenable. During that conversation, The One mentioned that #2 had said I was shirking my responsibilities, missing meetings, and was not clear about my role.

Fortunately for me (and because this was not my first time at the rodeo), I had receipts. I forwarded emails where #2 had explicitly told me not to attend certain meetings and to update logs about my work. When The One received that evidence, she said, "I'm aware #2 has some growth areas, but I support her."

Wow!

I felt my world crumble. Not only had I worked diligently for this organization, but a Black female leader had let me down. Despite her assurances that she wanted me in the organization and valued my work, her actions spoke otherwise. More than work, she and I had developed what I thought was a certain collegiality based on familial ties and time spent together outside the office. When I finally put it all together, her support for #2 was greater than her need to support me, and that hurt.

To barter for time, I told The One that taking a salary hit was unacceptable. I began meeting with the HR director to iron out what could be possible while deciding that it was time for me to be a consultant. I was honest about my moves, and six months later our divorce was final. I began consulting full-time in January 2021.

LESSONS

Ending any type of relationship is not easy. I mentioned previously that I felt off-kilter in this professional working relationship that was reminiscent of my personal relationships and was difficult to manage. I can reflect on the numerous negative harbingers, but my own sense of self, sense of purpose, faith, or simply my ego would not allow me to prepare for the inevitable. I honestly did not think I would have been offered a demotion. I didn't believe #2 would be so incredibly petty, and even if she was, I thought my relationship with The One would protect me. Not unlike in my personal life, I thought more of my relationship than the other person.

I had hoped that working on a large-scale grant with #2, even while she was creating a position and team for someone else, would have an impact on both of us. Part of my own, White-framed conditioning led me to believe that if I just worked harder, if I could just show #2 how dope I was, she would move away from her anti–Black female stance and recognize the gem that I obviously am. I allowed my sense of self-worth to create a blind spot as it related to this organization. #2 was so clearly done with me and wanted to prove to the rest of the organization what would happen if she was not in someone's corner. It would have been difficult to simply fire me; my work was too good, too many people knew me, and it could have left the organization open to a lawsuit. Instead, she chose to strip me of my title, move me to another department, and offer me $20K less—all while subtly indicating that I should somehow be grateful because jobs were scarce during the pandemic.

The real sting was that even though #2 orchestrated this entire situation, The One delivered the news. The One did not acknowledge the horrible situation and even shared lies #2 had fabricated to justify her actions. Perhaps most insidiously, The One allowed and encouraged #2's behavior, because there were no systems of accountability in place. Her support actively enabled #2 and was complicit in anti-Black-female toxicity. I later learned that other Black women who reported to #2 left the organization after I did—prompting me to wonder if the Black female–led organization was safe for Black women. Were there limits or constraints on The One of which I was unaware? What was the real relationship between #2 and The One that allowed them to uphold white supremacist patriarchy?

The courtship and marriage lasted three years, but the decision to cut ties with all organizations that do not value me is truly my place of freedom, where life, love, and leadership are allowed to flourish. I took a leap of faith, courage, and determination. I had no idea what it would yield, but I knew I could no longer allow people to try to dominate my brilliance. As Dr. Dillard (2021) says, I (re)membered WHO I am and Whose I am; I am "Black on purpose for a purpose" (p. 2).

I have created a Black Women affinity group series (see https://www.rachellerogersard.com/bw3l) for Black women to meet and share experiences. These cohorts of women help me further understand the necessity of safe spaces for Black women to be in proximity with one another. The groups meet four times per year (two in person, two remotely), and I facilitate the space in an effort to bring joy and healing to others.

Additionally, I have found through my consultancy the ability to draw on more than 27 years of work experience for organizations who want to do antiracist work while simultaneously creating space for writing, reading, walking, vacations, and eating good food. I choose the people with whom I work and say no to people and organizations that are not in alignment with my purpose. I do not chase the dollar; as I learned at the domino table when I was much younger, "all money ain't good money." I am also an executive coach who works only and unapologetically with Black women. While I enjoy spending time with non-Black women of color, I am intentional about who deserves my brilliance, my help, and my support. I am *Black on purpose for a purpose*, and my leadership experiences with shoddy White female leaders, wack Black female leaders, and non-Black female leaders of color who were intimidated by my brilliance have all led me to this point.

In the past I grappled with the duality of Dr. Rogers-Ard and 'Chelle; it has taken me a while to understand that, while different, both personalities are the dopeness that is Rachelle. I am Dr. Rogers-Ard in both professional and personal settings, just as sometimes it is necessary for 'Chelle to be present in both arenas. I used to hide 'Chelle the same way I would hide imperfection, thinking that if I showed up early, ready, with all work and charts neatly provided—with snacks—that somehow, those who were in senior positions would see my brilliance and create space for me at their table. It took a few instances of the table being denied, despite my mask of perfection, for me to understand that it was no use to hide 'Chelle; she was always there anyway, whispering in my ear and allowing me to show a little smirk when folks weren't watching. 'Chelle is as integral to my identity as Dr. Rogers-Ard, and I no longer hide her away—I understand perfection is an illusion.

In not hiding, I have reached a level of authenticity that I love! I am living, radically loving myself (Taylor, 2021), and finally understanding that my leadership reflects all that I am. I have written elsewhere about my HEART model for Authentic Leadership (Rogers-Ard & Knaus, 2020; see figure 5.1); I define leadership as "The deep understanding of oneself that forms the sum totality of one's personal life, empathy, perspectives and experiences" (Rogers-Ard & Knaus, 2020, p. 136). Leadership is "about knowing who you

Figure 5.1   Rogers-Ard Leadership Framework

are, how your past, present, and future life impacts how you are, and how you operate within systems of intersectional racism ... our leadership is our mirror and how we lead is a reflection of our values and lived experiences" (p. 136).

Living, loving myself radically, and being authentic in my leadership stance gives me the ability to move past people who are not good for my spirit for my own health and well-being. I name and call out negative characteristics within other people's leadership and revel in the freedom that leaving an unpleasant situation can give. I acknowledge those who are intimidated by my self-awareness, my poise, my brilliance, and my integrity. I acknowledge those who choose not to see the intersectional oppression I am faced with each working day. I acknowledge those whose internal demons are fighting with my internal godliness. And I say no. I say no as an act of resistance, as an act of self-love, and as a way to prioritize my health. I strive for a little more freedom each day. I live my life, practice radical self-love, and demonstrate authentic leadership. This is my new journey.

Chapter 6

The Audacity, Politics, and Pragmatism of Black Women's Leadership

Andrea E. Evans

In a 2019 *Forbes* magazine article titled, "Why Black Women Are Better Leaders," Dr. Paolo Gaudiano, a researcher on corporate diversity and inclusion, based his original premise on personal experiences and observations of "high-quality" Black women at professional events. Essentially, Gaudiano (2019) argued that while we might find more White leaders at higher levels of advancement, less-privileged groups who make it to those higher levels, on average, will have higher levels of innate talent. Further, he contended that having more White leaders at higher levels is not necessarily a reflection of their competence as much as it is a reflection of their privilege. Finally, Gaudiano hypothesized that "facing adversity tends to build character and increase competence—which would mean that disadvantaged people may have greater acquired skills in addition to greater innate talent" (para 15).

Such a public proclamation about Black women's skills and talent is both surprising and refreshing, even as his broader premise would not likely be widely believed or understood. Historically, Black women's position in American society has been fraught with pain, suffering, violence, hard work, caregiving (including forced caregiving), and a full array of racist and sexist acts and perceptions intended to diminish them as human beings. It should be widely known that Black women were once the "highest source of wealth during slavery" because they were "forced to produce wealth of slave masters through the birthing of new slaves" (Hughes, 2014, p. 19). Black women were, and often still are, caricatured as mammies, Jezebels, and angry. In the 1980s American politicians helped create the image of Black women as welfare queens, even as they worked outside the home in larger percentages than White women and more White women received public assistance. Yet, contrary to the societal stereotypes and narratives that have conveniently minimized or omitted their role in transforming the social, political, and economic aspects of American life, Black women have always been at the forefront of progress and change in this country.

Even with the "progress" that Black women have made in the decades since slavery and Jim Crow, they remain at risk at home and at school, in communities, and in the workplace. The double scourge of racism and misogyny continue to inflict various kinds of violence on Black women's minds, bodies, and psyches. For these reasons, I use the word *audacious* to characterize Black women leaders. Audacity refers to "boldness or daring, especially with confident or arrogant disregard for personal safety, conventional thought, or other restrictions (Dictionary.com, 2024). One need look no further than Judge Ketanji Brown Jackson's congressional confirmation hearing for the US Supreme Court to witness the kind of audacity that Black women often display as part of "progress." This country has now seen, for more than a century, the rise of Black women through the ranks of school and work, some even having the audacity to believe that they can lead and others will follow. As Elder (2022) so poignantly reminded us: "Black women keep moving forward because their dreams, ideas, and visions are greater than the forces trying to slow them down. Black women persist because they love their children, families, and communities. Black women persevere because they can" (p. 22).

We know that Black women have "a unique way of knowing and thinking about the world" (Bankole-Medina, 2021, p. 134). It should come as no surprise that Black women have special insights into the dangers that exist within society that threaten our collective freedom. For example, Black women acted together as the one voting bloc that overwhelmingly opposed Donald Trump in the 2016 election and held firm against him in 2020 to essentially save democracy. Black women's unique positionality as women and as a racial minority situates them to both see and experience our country and its institutions in ways that enable them to identify with pain, suffering, and inequality and to wield the strength, knowledge, and persistence to fight against them for the betterment of the whole of society. Black women have demonstrated the resilience and savvy to combat racism and sexism and to unleash their power, vision, voice, and authority to lead whenever and wherever they choose.

This chapter will explore the issues and challenges that Black women leaders must consider as they manifest the audacity and destiny to lead. I will examine this premise from several perspectives. First, I share some of the reasons Black women lead. Generally, Black women suggest that they lead in order to better understand oppression, out of a sense of duty, and/or as a form of activism, including renegotiating images of Black women. Also, I offer some of the traits, characteristics, and motivations Black women operationalize in order to manage their leadership and organizations. First, though,

I offer a brief discussion of Black women's quest for education as a possible connection to their abilities and pathways to leadership.

THE AUDACITY TO LEARN AND LEAD

To begin this examination of Black women's leadership, it is important to first acknowledge and center their respect for the need for education. Black women realized that ignorance doomed Black people to powerlessness (Epps, 2008). Initially left out of formal schooling, Black women saw education as the cornerstone of Black community development and pursued it for themselves and others through informal networks and strategies (Epps, 2008). Black women's formal education paths began long ago, but it is notable that the first Black females to receive PhDs all did so in 1921: Sadie Mossell Alexander, Eva Dykes, and Georgiana Simpson. These women and others paved the way for Black women seeking formal education to such a point that nearly 100 years later, there was much ado about Black women's pursuit of higher education. According to the American Association of University Women (AAUW, n.d.), by 2018, Black women were more likely than Black men to earn degrees. By then, they had earned 64% of bachelor's degrees, 72% of master's degrees, and 66% of doctoral, medical, and dental degrees.

However, Black women are far less likely than White women to enroll in four-year colleges, complete bachelor's degrees in six years, or receive advanced degrees (AAUW, n.d.). In 2020 the African American population was 12%, but only 8% of bachelor's degrees, 10% of master's degrees, 8.5% of academic doctorates, and 7% of professional doctorates were awarded. In fall 2020, however, Black people were 12% of all first-time graduate students, and 69% of them were women (AAUW, n.d.). Recently, we've witnessed declines in Black college student enrollment and completion, which was made worse by the pandemic of 2020. In 2010 there were 2.5 million Black college students; by 2020, it was down to 1.9 million (Adedoyin, 2022). Recent declines in Black community college students (down 18%, 15% for Black women) forecasts the diminished pipeline to four-year degree granting institutions, with possible negative implications for professional pathways to leadership (Adedoyin, 2022).

Having been open to Black leaders before other professional sectors (with K–12 education being one exception), the higher education sector provides a glimpse into the status of Black women leaders. Mary McCloud Bethune could be considered the first Black female university president. In 1904 she founded a boarding school called the Daytona Beach Literary and Industrial School for Training Negro Girls. This school later became a college and joined with the all-male Cookman Institute to become Bethune Cookman

College in 1923, which she led for 19 years. However, Willa Player is noted as the first African American woman to serve as president of a university, Bennett College, in 1956. In 2001 Dr. Ruth Simmons became the first African American woman to serve as president of an Ivy League school, Brown University. (It should be noted that it took until 2005 for a Black woman, Ursula Burns, to lead a Fortune 500 company.) We learn from the *American College President Study* (2017) that 30% of all college and university presidents were women; only 9% of them were Black. Of the 9% Black presidents, only 33% of them were Black women. While Black women have advanced, the data indicate that some conditions, circumstances, or mindsets may undermine their opportunity to reach to the highest levels of leadership in higher education, business, and other sectors.

WHY BLACK WOMEN LEAD

There is an inherent audacity in Black women's pursuit of leadership roles because of the dangers that racism and sexism present to them, as well as perceptions of who can and should lead (generally, White men). Yet there are some common themes that help explain why, despite the dangers, Black women forge ahead to take charge and take responsibility. For example, Bass (2009) explained that Black women have always sought to understand systems of oppression and who controlled and made the rules. This enabled them to navigate and function within the system they deemed as unjust to accomplish the purpose of helping those they care for. Similarly, Bankole-Medina (2021) suggested that Black women found that scholarly excellence and social responsibility were interchangeable, meaning that as Black women sought education, they knew they had a duty to serve, which was essential to Black survival and progress. Finally, according to Dillard (2016), Black women "lead with our lives," calling out the connection between their academic work and advocacy work, and as thinkers and sharers who choose to act (lead) in order to share (p. 31). It seems reasonable to suggest that for many Black women, leadership is, in fact, a calling.

Also, for Black women, leadership was and is a form of activism. Bass (2009) suggested that it is an "inherited legacy" (p. 620) that heightened perception and understanding of systems of oppression which provide the foundation for Black women's leadership. For example, Sales, Burke, and Cannonier (2020) argued that Black women knew they had a stake in the civil rights movement's success to "ensure their safety and their community from discrimination, social, and economic inequalities" (p. 355). Leadership and organizing provided the opportunity to empower themselves and their communities. Similarly, Epps (2008) found that Black women pursued leadership based on their belief in empowerment and sharing power within organizations.

Finally, as another form of activism, the preeminent Black feminist scholar Patricia Hill Collins (1986) argued that Black women should pursue leadership as a means to negotiate and reconcile images of Black women. Self-definition and self-evaluation are the ways in which Black women challenge externally defined stereotypical images of Black women. Placing themselves in leadership roles is an act of self-valuation—that is, by replacing externally driven images with authentic Black female images (Collins, 1986). Further, she suggested that self-definition validates Black women's power as human subjects. Self-valuation addresses the actual content of these self-definitions/distorted renderings of those aspects of Black female behavior seen as most threatening to White patriarchy. Collins (1986) advised women to embrace their assertiveness and use it to survive and thrive. Studies show that self-defined and self-valuing Black women populate the ranks of Black women leaders (Chance, 2021; Hughes, 2014; Jackson & Harris, 2007). As Black women pursue leadership opportunities and as they manage them, they make the choice to be self-defined and to eschew stereotypical images and perceptions of their abilities and their worth.

In addition to activism and social responsibility, some studies (Huang, 2017; Hughes, 2014) found that family and partner influence are important motivators for Black women's pursuit of leadership. Family members help Black women foster positive beliefs in their leadership capabilities. Hughes (2014) referenced "flexible life structures" (p. 23), which can be imagined in a variety of ways as necessary for Black women leaders, whether that involves expectations around traditional roles for Black women as caregivers or understanding the amount of time spent away from home for work or work travel. Huang (2017) found that women of color received validation and help overcoming self-doubt from their parents, enabling them to pursue leadership roles. Parents also reminded them of the responsibility toward their ethnic community. Further, Huang credited Black women's partners in pushing their spouses to take professional risks, interviewing for positions of leadership, and showing support of their careers. Finally, mentors played instrumental roles in connecting Black women to positions they might not otherwise consider or know about.

WHAT IT TAKES FOR BLACK WOMEN TO LEAD

As previously mentioned, the act of leadership for Black women can be a means to an end (both personal and social), but achieving those ends requires in-depth knowledge, unique and special skills, as well as personal traits such as self-efficacy. Self-efficacy is the personal belief that one can successfully perform an action or behavior. It is different than confidence, which can be nonspecific. Self-efficacy requires one to understand the tasks at hand and hold the belief that she has what it takes to be successful at those tasks. Hughes (2014) described career self-efficacy as one's capability to plan, implement, and execute a set of actions that yield certain career goals. This career self-efficacy results in positive career decisions that are enabled by competence in five career choice areas—self-appraisal, occupational information, goal selection, problem-solving, and planning—and by a mature attitude regarding career choice process. Competence in these areas, along with the mature attitude, manifests as internal sources of strength and power, which may be just as important, if not more important, than positional power for Black women in leadership positions (Hughes, 2014).

Chance (2021) described crucible experiences as adverse and transformational experiences which served as "trials in shaping leadership development" for Black women (p. 617). Those experiences provided points of "deep reflection that required women to question who they were and what mattered to them, examining their values, questioning their assumptions, and honing their judgments. As such, crucible experiences caused women to emerge stronger and surer of themselves and their purpose" (p. 617). Those experiences promoted their resilience and helped them "survive and thrive" (p. 617) rather than "plateau or dissipate" (p. 618).

One cannot overstate the importance of emotional intelligence needed by Black women leaders. Hughes (2014) offered a poignant statement on this trait for Black women:

> American Black women are emotionally intelligent, but they are astute enough to not disclose that they recognize the body language, the tones of condescension, and the outright disrespect expressed against them within society and at work. They are judged to lack emotional intelligence by others who are not at all emotionally intelligent enough to recognize their emotional intelligence. It is absurd to expect American Black women in leadership positions to not be emotionally intelligent. Their very survival to achieve a leadership position is because they are emotionally intelligent enough to assimilate to the cultural norms to the extent necessary to attain a leadership position. They had to survive insults at every level of their educational experience and on every job and interaction on the job. They are treated as if they are brand new to the world when they begin a new position in the workplace. All of their experiences are irrelevant or unimportant because they are expected to do only what they are told or allowed to do and not to think for themselves. If they do think for themselves, they are expected to seek the validation of others before their thoughts can be accepted as real or relevant. (p. 89)

This statement surfaces the underlying diminution of Black women who have ascended to leadership positions. In other words, Black women can and do possess the types of credentials, dispositions, and experiences to get the job, yet they endure a second level of disregard and disrespect that minimizes all of who they are, what they know, and what they brought to the organization in the first place. To be clear, Black women leaders may receive this type of treatment from other Black folks, including other Black women. Due to the normalized oppression that undergirds American society and its institutions, racist and sexist assaults on Black women can manifest in the actions of persons of any race and any gender.

For these and many other reasons, it is safe to say that, out of sheer necessity, Black women develop a leadership style that is all their own, both as individuals and with some common characteristics with and among Black women. As suggested earlier, Black women's self-authorship (see Kegan, 1982) expands their capacity to generate their own beliefs, identity, and relationships toward an ability to influence others. Further, the self-authorship concept suggests that Black women come to know their own minds and have confidence that they can be effective decision-makers for organizations.

As part of their self-authorship, there are some specific characteristics, traits, and skills Black women leaders need. Holder, Jackson, and Ponterotto (2015) suggested that Black women acquire coping strategies and are savvy in gathering cues from their environment by paying attention to interpersonal dynamics in the workplace. The ability to diagnose and process experiences of racial microaggressions can protect Black women from internalizing the negative impact of these incidents. Also, it presents opportunities to flex and strengthen their strategic and decision-making skills in the workplace and opportunities to enhance their self-awareness abilities and overall emotional intelligence (Holder et al., 2015).

In addition, Black women, who can be criticized for being overconfident or arrogant, must interact with and navigate others' attitudes and behaviors in a work environment designed for them to fail. They may deal with maltreatment from others and endure a hostile work environment, which may include the lack of personnel and resources. They must ignore all of the subjectively designed systems and constraints used against them by peers, leaders, and subordinates, even as they are often expected to provide more evidence of their competence in order to prove themselves (Gardner, Barrett, & Pearson, 2014). Further, Gardner et al. (2014) argued that Black women must overcome tokenism, which affects their authority and achievement in organizations and systems. Finally, Black women cannot and should not be timid when expressing their viewpoint as they find and share their voice. They must always aim to be prepared and professional.

Without question, the racial climate of many organizations calls for higher standards of behavior for Black women compared to other races and genders (Gardner et al., 2014). Further, expectations that others have may be different than what Black women might have for themselves. It is within this context that Black women can find space to self-define, thrive, and guide organizations to effectively address, respond to, and embed diversity, equity, and inclusion as part of the organizational culture and its practices. Black women can articulate diversity and pursue platforms for organizations that align with their missions and the unique realities of a multicultural society (Epps, 2008). In this way, Black women exhibit their unique power to instruct, inform, and transform organizations into spaces that are safe for them, for those who look like them, and for other marginalized groups. As they have throughout history, Black women must use the levers of change at their disposal to exhibit their cultural competence and utilize their cultural capital as a means to advance organizations toward equity, inclusion, fairness, and justice.

CONCLUSION

Black women's place in American society is a complex story of pain and suffering, empowerment and promise, service and leadership, within and outside of the Black community. The perceptions of Black women remain mixed, with stereotypes holding firm amid a plethora of Black women leaders operating behind the scenes and out front in the media, business, politics, the arts, sciences, and in sectors such as higher education. Yet Black women bring their own rich perspectives and a strong sense of self to any space they inhabit. The dual identities of marginalized people, their Blackness and their womanhood, give them a worldview like no other, one that uniquely positions them as leaders. It is within their intersectionality that their power lies. As Elder (2022) stated, "to wield power like a black woman is to identify a goal, dream, or desire, then work toward it with persistence, confidence, patience" (p. 170). Our society and our democracy depend on Black women's willingness to wield that power.

Chapter 7

This Too Shall Pass, or Will It?

Roxane L. Gervais and Yetunde Ade-Serrano

OUR REALITY

Having a title such as "This Too Shall Pass, or Will It?" within the context of "A Woman Will Manifest" feels a bit odd to conceptualize. What it does is establish this chapter in our realities, in the expression of our actions, in the choices we make as Black women holding leadership roles, and in the lived experiences of questioning and challenging the shifting platforms that propose to hold the weight of our integrities.

For me, Roxane, identity is important. There are those who see and choose to identify me as a Black woman, which I am; nonetheless, that is not all I am. It is but a fragment of my reality. There are visual and vocal aspects of how I am perceived that do not resonate with the beliefs I hold true for myself. The resulting dissonance from the rejection of such perceptions has, at times, left me questioning, "Who am I?" The answers are not contained in the limited labeling bestowed by my environment and circumstances, but in how I negotiate my world and ascribe meaning to my experiences. I hold onto my ancestry, its fusion and multiculturalism, to ground me against the many challenges I encounter. I reflect on those strong women who defined my ancestral heritage in their actions, growth, and focus against adversity, which allow me to resonate on my experiences, accepting that life is not static and that change is inevitable.

I, Yetunde, choose to describe myself in the way that the spirit of God directs. Meaning that in the real moments of realization, the who I am is not rapt by the entities of the world. In defiance against the perception of others or the confinement such perceptions bring, I choose to designate myself as a child of the world. In my reality, I am not defined by time or space or color, but by the presence of today, yesterday, tomorrow, and the places those before me have inhabited and continue to occupy. I am defined by the breath of life, the breast I suckle, and the milk of the mother that flows to nourish and sustain. Sometimes it is about living in the moment, often consumed by the past and the longing for a different reality. Part of this means I experience pain, hurt, and joy among other emotions and the pride of being a Black woman.

We consider, "Who am I?" As we reflect on this question, we share how we traverse this part of ourselves, the Black women who stand up to be counted (occasionally not consciously so), the internal and external framework of our functioning, including the power and privilege we hold, and the junctions that give us pause at the same time as our individual determinations and tenacity to shift narratives.

In this chapter we attempt to explore how we started, why we chose the paths we trekked, and, perhaps more significantly, we endeavor to unveil that which we have hidden as a means to survive.

We are two "Black" women—an identifier that, while it is useful and succinct, does not fully encompass us as women, as leaders, as individuals who have made, continue to make, tried to make, and can make a difference. It is an identifier that at times does not represent our competence, expertise, leadership skills, and abilities. While we accept this identifier, we question it as we take account of and nurture our leadership capabilities.

THE OVERLAPS OF GENDER AND SKIN COLOR WITH BEING A LEADER

As leaders, especially as Black women who lead, we remain cognizant of the elements of our lives that intersect. This awareness of the presence of intersectionality as it relates to Black women and our experiences has become more prominent. It benefits us by encouraging, ourselves and others, to consider a more holistic understanding of those attributes that impact our individuality. Crenshaw (1989, 1991), in defining intersectionality, advocated for the need to account for multiple identities to frame and better understand the social sphere. The first section in this chapter saw us outlining "Our Reality," which embodies our intersectional selves. We cannot step away from who we are even in our leadership roles; we are who we are. Our leadership experiences require that we contend with prevailing stereotypes regarding our competence at leading due to our gender and race (see, e.g., Sanchez-Hucles & Davis, 2010). We are more likely to be seen as Black women, with the one-drop rule fully in effect (Sweet, 2005), despite our ancestry and how we choose to define who we are. This is especially true when we enter that space as leaders with retaining expectations of what that means in terms of color (race) and gender. Consequently, we are challenged on the basis of this narrow focus.

The numerous stereotypes associated with gender, race, and ethnicity leave Women of Color who are in leadership roles more likely to be subjected to a three-way risk of not being accepted in their roles (Sanchez-Hucles & Sanchez, 2007). This nonacceptance works to contain our—Black women's—identities, including our gender and race, ignoring our place of birth and often the languages we speak, which may not be limited to English (Sanchez-Hucles & Sanchez, 2007). We are multifaceted but are usually contained within a box of what is most comfortable for those with whom we interact. Our—Women of Color—multifaceted ethnic and racial backgrounds support our ability to project self-confidence and independence, to use direct communication, and to overall exercise stronger influencing strategies than those used by women who present with European backgrounds (Parker & Ogilvie, 1996). I, Roxane, was raised in a multilingual, cultural, racial, and religious society, with all the traits defining us as us, with relatives and friends across all of those spectrums, where differences were the norm. In that environment, I was used to working with and interacting with People of Color in leadership positions and being accepted as a leader, solely due to the position and not the person. Leadership requires influencing followers with a focus on the leader's position, power, and authority (Yukl, 2013), but the existence of stereotypical views can limit Black women's ability to influence effectively in their leadership roles.

We have confidence in stating what we can do and what we have accomplished as leaders. However, this has at times not been to our benefit. As women, we promote ourselves at the risk of losing our position but with the prospect to influence and progress as leaders (Eagly & Carli, 2007). For example, I, Yetunde, recalled one scenario in which I enforced ethical practice and kept firm on my boundaries for the benefit of the community being served, while ensuring that I nurtured my team. I was confident in sharing the changes I implemented with the senior management team. Consequently, I faced challenges regarding my professional capabilities and my actions as a leader, resulting in my concluding my term prematurely. In another example, I, Roxane, led a large project with impact at European and international levels for five years. I did the groundwork for the project and ensured a highly supportive and financed project. When the project became more prominent and more visible, I was accused of poor leadership and chairing by the other members of the team, all individuals who identified as White men and women. In one instance I was physically threatened, ironically at a social event; in another I was strongly asked to step back from the role and to take on a junior role. I refused. I was subsequently removed from the role by the other members and replaced by a White man. These incidents are reflected in

Eagly and Carli's (2007) observation that "some impediments are not subtle. Worse of all, by depicting a single, unvarying obstacle, the glass ceiling fails to incorporate the complexity and variety of challenges that women can face in their leadership journeys" (p. 64). We would state that the challenges, inherent with their complexity and variety, we experience in our leadership roles change daily and collide with different parts of the system that do not work to our benefit.

Our experiences are not an aberration but expose the reality for many Black women who seek and engage in leadership roles. Women, inclusive of Black women, are less likely to attain leadership positions, to remain on leadership tracks, and therefore less likely to become leaders (Eagly & Carli, 2007).

INCLUSION AND ANTI-RACISM AS THE FIX FOR BLACK WOMEN'S LEADERSHIP

It is widely accepted that embracing inclusion and anti-racism are essential practices and beliefs in ensuring fairness (see "Chartered Institute of Personnel and Development" [CIPD], 2021; European Commission, 2020). While a certain level of awareness of these constructs can modify perceptions, the various challenges required to attain fully inclusive and anti-racist organizations can make this outcome seem untenable.

The literature stipulates that these types of initiatives are inconsistent and less likely to achieve their goals (see, e.g., Dobbin et al., 2015; Dobusch, 2021; Dover et al., 2020; Eagly & Koenig, 2021). As noted, inclusion must occur at the individual level and is better facilitated when both belongingness and uniqueness (see, e.g., Shore et al., 2011) can be achieved within a group or organizational setting. It is interesting to question the relevance of these two facets for Black women as leaders within a professional context. In reality, the likelihood of our retaining our uniqueness while at the same time feeling that we belong within an organizational setting, to influence our followers solely as Black women, is low. The uniqueness referenced in the opening paragraphs of this section will have to consider the intersection of our identifications and the resultant systemic impacts on our lives. Equally, our sense of belongingness is built on a foundation that does not account for the uniqueness we bring to our leadership roles. Notably, despite significant progress in raising awareness about intersectionality, diversity, inclusion, and belonging, the actual organizational shifts recommended by these advances have yet to be achieved. It is worth noting that outside of theoretical contexts and guidelines, the use of inclusion and anti-racist practices is limited to lip servicing.

We would like to think we have retained (most) of our uniqueness in our leadership roles but have sometimes struggled in our belongingness to the groups and the organizations in which we lead or have led. Despite this disconnect, we have strived to add value in the way we have navigated the leadership roles. For example, we tend to bring as much of ourselves as is needed to fulfill the roles, therefore maintaining our authentic sense of self. We are introverts and can present with ambivert behaviors if any of our roles require that we take a strong stance, use a firm and forceful voice, or take a decision that is required but one with which not everyone will agree. We know we are leading, but our actions can be interpreted as those of the pervasive "angry Black woman." We are seen as less communal but more agentic (see, e.g., Rosette et al., 2016). Of course it is established that when men lead, they should be assertive, dominant, and forceful, but when women engage in similar behaviors, these traits are seen as unacceptable (Eagly & Carli, 2007). For us, there is a balance to be had in not succumbing to the demands of silencing from others. On the one hand, we cultivate nurturing and potentially appear as mothering figures, which can leave us carrying the weight of tasks. Our value to all leadership roles is grounded in the relationships we create with those we engage and serve. These can include junior members of our teams who have expressed gratitude for how we lead, interact with them, support them, and ensure they develop from the relationship.

It could be said that there is inconsistency in progressing inclusion and anti-racism policies, practices, and procedures within organizations. While the value and/or requirement for these are generally accepted, it is likely that these initiatives rely on persons of color *fixing* the issues or being asked or volunteered to implement them (Nance-Nash, 2020). In one recent incident, I, Yetunde, was asked whether I knew what I was talking about when discussing the "single narrative" that was being propagated regarding the impact of COVID-19 on Black communities, while at the same time being asked indirectly to be the "face" that bridges the gap between "us" and "them." Additionally, I, Roxane, have been asked on various occasions to provide context for "Black" and "ethnic" concerns.

THE REALITY OF IMPOSTER SYNDROME

We feel quite capable of using our leadership skills. All individuals lead at some point in their lives, although they may not necessarily accept that their actions and behaviors are those that constitute leadership practices. As Black women, we step up when we see the need for leadership in our work and personal lives, and we do not feel uncomfortable doing so. Despite our confidence in our capabilities and capacities to function as leaders, we have found that others may try to impose their perceptions of imposter syndrome on our abilities. Imposter syndrome has become a de rigueur explanation of women's "shortcomings" within the workplace, regardless of their veracity.

It is useful to acknowledge that the term *imposter syndrome* emerged from Clance and Imes's (1978) imposter phenomenon construct, which has been described as "an internal experience of intellectual phoniness" (Clance & Imes, 1978, p. 241). Taking account of the widespread use of the term, Tulshyan and Burey (2021) encourage managers to reassess their interpretation of imposter syndrome—to not interpret those natural human reactions of self-doubt, hesitation, and lack of confidence as anything other than what they are, which is a human phenomenon that questions one's own sense of achievement and success. Individuals will manage the best they can, with the resources that are available to them. In our experience, the imposter syndrome is used as a weapon to demotivate and diminish Black women leaders because of how plausible the concept is; that is, it is very real and is often situated in a lot of people's lives. It is not unique to Black women. However, when this concept is projected onto Black women, who would have more likely than not had a history of discrimination, the phenomenon can become exacerbated, leading to an affirmation of White system stereotypes.

In this respect, while our self-image is one of being strong, effective, and competent, we can be perceived as being weak, ineffective, and incompetent, thereby being labeled as suffering from imposter syndrome. We are therefore questioned consistently on what we do, why we do it, and how we do it. This is despite obtaining good outcomes, such as Roxane successfully leading a European project for eight years. This involved managing staff and subprojects, assessing the performance of team members, addressing any issues that arose, delivering quality outputs, and being the face of the organization. Each year saw the creation of new multidisciplinary teams, which would involve leading diverse teams in up to eight countries, with from 5 to 15 collaborators in each team. My strong leadership, management, and effective decision-making increased the annual income each year, culminating in a fourfold increase at the end of the eighth year. This outcome reflects much better outcomes than those with whom I worked, for example, White colleagues delivering lower outputs, refusing to do more than one or two projects at the same time, or refusing to take on a project that was assigned as within their expertise. As People and Women of Color, when our work performance is evaluated, this is less on what we have done and how well we have done it and more on how we look (i.e., as Black and women). Furthermore, our performance is attributed to luck or exceptional effect rather than to our skills and abilities (Tackey et al., 2001). This was applied to my, Roxane's, leadership of the European project. However, when I stepped aside, I continued to support the project, as those who were assigned to do so struggled to understand what was required to manage it, and the process of managing it, effectively.

As Black women who lead, we realize we engage in code switching (McCluney et al., 2019). This can be automatic. Most of the time we are aware when these shifts occur. On reflection, perhaps we use this technique to challenge the concept of imposter syndrome in that we assess the situation to determine the response that is needed. This could include using standard English in a precise tone, whether on the phone or in person; having an increased awareness of the cultural aspects of the situation depending on the diversity of the person(s) with whom we are interacting; and knowing when we can divert to more informal language, dialect, or accent.

The imposter syndrome can manifest not necessarily at a particular junction of doubt but often, in our experience, during quiet contemplation and impromptu moments, such as walking down the supermarket aisle wondering which detergent to settle for, as the supermarket has run out of the "normal one." For us, the identifier of Black woman leader was not born out of a meditated process for fame or fortune (this is one perception) or for center stage recognition (another perception); nor was it from the need to influence or have followers, as the definition of *leader* might indicate (Hassanzadeh et al., 2015). It comes perhaps from knowing that when we want to shift something, we can, that we have the vision and the drive to see it through. We are reminded as individuals that our self-definition as Black professional women (Ade-Serrano, 2010) is embedded in our internalization of experiences.

In Ade-Serrano's (2010) research project, participants explored the meaning of their self-definition and individuality within the context of their work and personal lives. They considered how their sense of selves was maintained through negotiating multiple parts of self, by contemplating whether their individuality was integrated into their self-view. This process involved deliberating the relationship one has with herself, with others, and within the multiple roles each participant held. Contrary to previous research in this area, Ade-Serrano's research project highlights the role of choice and conflict in the construction and maintenance of the self, which can have implications for how Black women work. These findings suggest that its participants wrestle to consciously comprehend the dynamics between internal and external discourses, thereby concluding that Black women's self-definition and individuality are premised "not as a symptom of social deviance but as a strategy in response to the exercise of choice" (p. 220). It is our sense of self that battles the imposter syndrome police.

USING OUR RESOURCES

We rely on our resilience to continue to function in our leadership roles. The nature of the consistent challenge is disconcerting, especially when it does not lead to a positive outcome. Rather, it functions as a distraction from effective leading. As stated in "The Reality of Imposter Syndrome" section, we have a vision, and our task in all roles is to see the vision created. It is useful for us, as Black women who choose to continue to lead despite continuous setbacks, to explore if we have become inured to these challenges. Of course we accept that as Black women we are more likely to receive challenges in our leadership roles (Kramer, 2020), and that we are evaluated more negatively than Black men, White women, and White men (Rosette & Livingston, 2012).

Burey (2020) suggests that Black women should not bring their authentic self to the workplace, as our authentic selves—e.g., hair, language, dress—will not fit into the wider and dominant organizational culture. This can lead to our being questioned in terms of why an action was taken or not taken. There will not be a "right" answer to what we do and why we did it, as our abilities, competencies, and authentic selves will be seen as less than.

The demonstration of Black women as leaders encompasses the unified whole of who we are. Therefore, our essence is embodied in the roles we choose to step up to or step into. We reflect on Audre Lorde's (2007/2021) powerful words:

> Those of us who are poor, who are lesbians, who are Black, who are older—know that survival is not an academic skill. It is learning how to take our differences and make them strengths. For the master's tools will never dismantle the master's house. They may allow us temporarily to beat him at his own game, but they will never enable us to bring about genuine change. And this fact is only threatening to those women who still define the master's house as their only source of support. (p. 112)

These words allow us to consider that the determination of us as Black women individually, and possibly collectively, assures us that our intentions and choices are some of the resources we utilize in navigating our world as leaders. We pay homage to the entirety of existence, whether consciously or unconsciously, in fulfilling such roles, acknowledging that there will be shortcomings and successes in delivering objectives. As the Gambian proverb suggests, "If you want to go fast, go alone. If you want to go far, go together." We navigate through doing it alone and doing it with others, mindful of the damage that can emerge from either of the processes.

We propose that some of the systemic resources available to support our endeavors as leaders do not add value or assist us with what we want to achieve as leaders—the system, in creating organizational policies that drive practices, serves itself. For example, consider management systems that are skewed toward specific individuals—the ones more likely to have access to information, to have control, and to be rewarded. A system that is inherently racist does not promote the work of People of Color. Is it therefore problematic to assert that the system does not ensure that we have appropriate resources to allow us to deliver our objectives? Of course we would argue that it is a necessity. In so doing, however, we risk minimizing our sense of self. The act of questioning the organization's power generates negative perceptions around our overlapping intersections of gender and race.

We would posit further that systemic resources, such as socialization, team-building, employee development, and empowerment programs, are normally centered on a Westernized view of the world, and thus the organization is less likely to be accepting of ideas not perceived from the Westernized vantage point. We acknowledge that some individuals contained within these organizations are considered diverse (i.e., non-White), thus providing a disguise for the racial and cultural dynamics that undermine equity. Consequently, we are left doing a balancing act between our internalized frameworks, which can also be sometimes fractured, and the external environment. The resulting phenomenon in these unsupportive systems and environment is the overreliance on the internal human and cultural resources, which have the potential to deplete us. The systemic changes that are needed must be systematic (Yukl, 2013), that is, well thought out, structured, and encompassing.

We have often found that we needed to dig deep, more times than we can count, to retrieve those resilient internal resources to continue in leadership roles. We have had to reflect, re-center, reenergize, because for us there was a purpose to our leadership journey. Not fulfilling that purpose means the experiences we have had to endure were for nothing. As we write this, we do wonder whether this reflection feeds into the socialization of us as Black women. Is a journey ever "nothing"?

On occasion, we get the question of "Why do you do what you do?" from younger women psychologists. This can be an uplifting experience because it reminds us of how a woman will manifest. In turn, we hope our visibility as leaders can inspire other Women of Color to take up the mantle of leadership as, at this juncture, we remember the Gambian proverb and know we no longer walk alone.

THINGS THAT WORK FOR US

- *Having a consistent and strong support system.* We are privileged to have friends and colleagues outside of the workspace in whom to confide. We are

able to disclose our true and raw feelings, and in these spaces we are seen, heard, and held. We spend time with family and friends and pursue those activities that calm our spirits.
- *Setting boundaries.* We set boundaries around the activities of our leadership roles. For example, prioritizing the work at hand, over people wanting to disrupt the work, and ensuring clear communication processes are in place.
- *Upskilling others.* We upskill the support we have, for example, administrative support, to allow them to move forward with many issues without our having to sign off on every action. Further, as administrative support is generally done by women, we are developing their skill set, building their confidence, and thereby teaching them to lead.
- *Trusting ourselves.* We have a strong sense of self, which allows us to either not respond to detractors, or take our time in deciding how to respond to them. We developed the ability, strength, and focus to speak our minds and not replicate the silence imposed by organizations.

WE RETURN TO THE QUESTION, WILL IT PASS?

So, what are the next steps in our leadership journey? The "call for more sophisticated and multifaceted definitions of race and other dimensions of identity" (Sanchez-Hucles & Davis, 2010, p. 179) is not new. It may change at some point, or may never change, and this should not hinder Black women from taking on leadership roles. We have advanced and made a difference as leaders, despite the numerous obstacles we have faced.

As this chapter closes, we return to our initial question: "Will it pass?"

In an age where we thirst for equity both within society and organizations, we contend that it will not pass, though there is optimism in a shifting world. Our attempt at addressing the barriers of progress and manifesting who we are may mean our voices will remain not unheard but ignored. However, one "fix," according to Woods et al. (2022), is through coalition building, our ability to create, maintain, and sustain ourselves through relationships with similar "others," feeding these others while equally getting fed.

Another potential way forward is not to contribute to the power minimization of ourselves—to not allow the power we have to be minimized to nothingness and/or insignificance. We must also not accept it or continue to bathe in its glory of affirmation. This is because we know who we are and what we are. We are strong Black women who lead and make a difference to people and processes. We expect challenge, as leaders should be challenged, but the challenge has *to be relevant, to lead to a stronger outcome than the one we were pursuing*, and *to contribute to a legacy*. Unfortunately, most of our challenges to date have not followed those precepts, as the focus has been on us as Black women, not on us leaders who happen to be Black women.

We reflect on why we chose to do so. We ask, "Has it served a purpose?" And "What is this purpose?" While this was difficult for us to do in parts because it has felt exposing, we have memorialized these experiences by sharing them in this way. We would have preferred to be treated fairly as leaders, ensuring that this minimization had never materialized. Our connection to "A Woman Will Manifest" was the trigger to remind us of the relationship we have to each other; in particular, the experiences we have shared. Our hope is to inspire and reaffirm that we, and other Black women, are not less than. We recognize the declaration of Mary Barnett in upholding our worth as unique individuals as we attest, "I am. I stand in my own being, no matter what" (Wignot, 2021, 54:28–54:36).

For us, this chapter serves that purpose. We want to encourage other Black women, bearing in mind individual intersectional facets, to be more accepting of the mantle of leadership. Often, you are doing it already! Therefore, we advocate that you can lead, that you do lead—and that when someone challenges your leadership, it usually is not because you cannot lead and are not making an impact, but that others see your leadership as a threat and know they cannot, or struggle to, stand in their own being.

Part III

A MORE RADICAL ELSEWHERE
Whitneé Garrett-Walker

As we offer our final section, we offer examples of the freedom possible through Black women's leadership. We offer reflections in the form of radical dreaming and love letters that seek to bring forth a new way of engaging ourselves and our commitments to healing as Black women. Our reflection offerings serve as an entry point into the field of leadership for Black women who are currently in the field, and for Black women who are yet to come. A more radical elsewhere is the space created for us by our trailblazing ancestors who've led movements that have given us the very freedom, literature, and connection we currently have. Therefore we offer this section through a lens of Afro-Futuristic promise where Black women speak life into one another through a liberatory transcendence of time.

Chapter 8

Keisha vs. Karen

We Ain't Doing This No More!

Renée Heywood and Rhema Heywood

School is a hyperviolent space for Black students and in particular for Black girls. Black girls continue to be adultified, criminalized, and spirit-murdered by educators who enact racially discriminatory school disciplinary policies (Hines & Wilmot, 2018). According to the National Center for Education Statistics (2022), the percentage of White teachers slightly decreased from 84% to 79% percent between 1999 and 2018. In 18 years we should have seen more progress in the diversification of educators, but instead changes in the data are insignificant. Because 76% of educators are women, children are more likely to have a White female teacher than a teacher of color or a male. This means that Black girls and boys have few role models in the field of education and are rarely able to see reflections of themselves in positions of leadership in academic spaces. It is important that Black children have these role models so they too can aspire to make an impact on the institution of education.

Over the past decade, Black boys have been the target of disproportionate discipline in schools, but now attention is turning to the harsh treatment of Black girls for seemingly different expectations of their behavior compared to their White peers. According to recent research, teachers view Black girls as more suspicious, mature, and aggressive than their White peers and are punished more frequently, for example, for violating dress codes (Green et al., 2020). If schools are teaching curricula that have erased the presence of Black females from the heroic narrative of American exceptionalism (save for a few references during Black History Month in February), are they not implicitly constructing a narrative of exclusion? In a world of normalized exclusion, how and where, then, do Black girls situate themselves as Americans and as global citizens (Morris, 2016)?

Decentering whiteness requires that educators develop spirit-healing pedagogies that acknowledge the racialized and gendered violence Black girls encounter in school while engaging in reparative acts of resistance to the white supremacist structures that dehumanize Black girls. However, dismantling anti-Black aggressive behaviors and spirit-murdering should not occur *after* an educator has inflicted irreparable harm (Hines & Wilmot, 2018). It is important to educate White teachers and administrators of the harm caused through the various assaults on the dignity of Black students. Racial oppression is a traumatic form of interpersonal violence which can lacerate the spirit, scar the soul, and puncture the psyche. Without a clear and descriptive language to describe this experience, those who suffer cannot coherently convey their pain, let alone heal (Hardy, 2013). Relating this term to an academic setting may seem extreme to some; however, it expresses the damage done through our educational system that, from its inception, has been laced with racism, causing harm within the classroom and school environment. Youth of color are affected by oppressive curricula and pedagogy.

To foster spirit-healing, schools must also eradicate disciplinary policies that promote the spirit-murdering of Black girls at the expense of what Dumas (2007) refers to as the Black educational imagination. For Black and Brown children in the United States, a major part of their schooling experience is associated with White female teachers who have no understanding of their culture. That was certainly my experience in K–12 schooling that was filled with White teachers who, at their core, were good people but unknowingly were murdering my spirit with their lack of knowledge, care, and love of my culture (Love, 2019). Garcia and Davila (2021) refer to Bettina Love's definition of *spirit murdering* as "a slow death, a death of the spirit, a death that is built on racism intended to reduce, humiliate and destroy people of color" (p. 4). Hines and Wilmot (2018) propose that "Black girls have an educational imagination that should account for the racial and gendered nature of emancipatory freedoms that Black girls are denied in school." They suggest that "spirit-healing must center the revolutionary power of the educational imagination of Black girlhood" (p. 68).

I have witnessed an attempt to dim the light of our Black girls coupled with cultural invasion, which is a poisonous cocktail that causes their trauma. Paulo Freire (2000) said more than 50 years ago something that still resonates with me today: "This phenomenon, the invaders penetrate the cultural context of another group, in disrespect of the latter's potentialities; they impose their own view of the world upon those they invade and inhibit the creativity of the invaded by curbing their expression" (p. 152). This happens every day in classrooms where Black culture is viewed as a deficit, Black language is a marker for less intelligence, and our Black students are not able to experience their childhood because they are not viewed as having the same innocence as their White peers. They are affected by the implicit biases, racial socialization, and power that are manifested through microaggressions and the devaluation of who they are (Heywood, 2021). These are the biases and stereotypes that result in the institutional failure that pushes Black children into the school-to-prison pipeline.

Research from Epstein and colleagues (2017) refers to three dominant paradigms of Black femininity that originated in the South during the period of slavery and have persisted into present-day culture—paradigms that "paint Black females as hypersexual, boisterous, aggressive, and unscrupulous": (1) Sapphire (emasculating, loud, aggressive, angry, stubborn, and unfeminine); (2) Jezebel (hypersexualized, seductive, and exploiter of men's weaknesses); and (3) Mammy (self-sacrificing, nurturing, loving, asexual) (p. 5). These images and historical stereotypes of Black women have serious consequences for Black girls today and are threats that keep Black girls in a matrix of domination, seen as something to be controlled and not worthy of positive attention. Black girls deserve to shine and not be relegated to roles that are defined by stereotypes. They are beautiful, complex, and have layered identities that are an asset to their learning environment and community. The counter-narrative must be told so that they can experience true freedom and can be seen for the precious gems they are, because education needs them to assume their rightful place as educators and leaders.

The following poem is a conversation between a Black mother and her daughter about the challenges of being a Black girl in school. The Black girl is represented by the name Keisha as a proxy for those who are negatively affected by their White female teachers, represented by the name Karen. In the past few years, as racial tensions have been televised and shared on social media, the term *Karen* has been created to describe a White woman who uses her whiteness and privilege as a means to control situations where Black people have the audacity to thrive. Black students are starting to use the name Karen to describe their White female teachers who misuse their power in the classroom and in the schoolhouse through daily assaults on the dignity of their Black students. Black girls are often the subject of attention when it comes to dress code violations and discipline. Writing for the Georgetown Law Center on Poverty and Inequality, Epstein et al. (2017) reported that Black girls between the ages of 5 and 14 are seen as "less innocent and more adult-like than white peers" (p. 13), and this adultification peaks between ages 10 and 14. Black girls are being chastised and criminalized for meritless infractions, including having "too much attitude," chewing gum too loudly, and talking "unladylike" (Hines & Wilmot, 2018, p. 63).

This poem gives Keisha the opportunity to reimagine education by disrupting racist ideologies and re-centering transformational education through her counter-narrative. The reader is able to hear the voice of Black girls through

Keisha, their representative, and see themselves in one of the three characters portrayed here. The reader who identifies closely with Karen should be moved through self-reflection, empathy, and humility to make changes to how they treat their students of color, in particular Black girls. The reader who identifies closely with the mother should be encouraged to continue their role as a cheerleader, hero, and champion for their Black children. The reader who identifies with Keisha should feel a sense of validation in this poem while also feeling empowered to speak truth to power in order to disrupt racist practices in education. In this chapter we imagine a world where the Keishas of the world can speak to the Karens of the world and say, "Enough is enough! We ain't doing this no more!"

Keisha:
Hey, Mom, can I ask you something? How old do I look today?
And don't say 25, because then I'll feel some kind of way.
Hey, Mom, why does my teacher always ask me about the boys?
She always feels the need to remind me to not let them touch my toys.
I told her that they approached me, but she gave me a weird explanation.
She said it's because I look experienced, isn't that adultification?
Adultification is racial prejudice against Black and Brown girls like me,
But I am the same age as everyone else, can't Ms. Karen see?
Why do I constantly have to defend my innocence?
And why do I always have to prove being sneaky is never my intent?
I just see things differently and ask certain questions.
But why when I know the right answers do I still feel less than?
I mean, they expect me to know everything, but sometimes I'm just maintaining.
But having to be the adult of the group is in fact quite draining.
And, Mom, this dress code is not for me.
How do they expect me to sit comfortably
while maintaining the appropriate but trendy themes?
I mean Becky gets away with it, they walk past her and leave her alone.
But what am I supposed to do, leave my spice and curves at home?
They just don't understand that my swag and fashion takes up space.
But sometimes my big curly and coiled hair makes me feel so out of place.
But, see, they always take my trends and try to wear my street wear too.
But, baby, you don't got the hood behind the hoops; only my sisters do.
But just because some days I'm hood doesn't mean I am not classy.
I could rock ripped jeans one day and the next satin slacks as you walk right past me.
But I never understood my teachers every time I pop out in my drip.
It's like they forget I'm a kid, even though they never treat me like it.

Mom:
Just like Apple Beats said, "You love Black Culture, but do you love me?"

which checks those
who believe they can steal our culture but still devalue us as human beings.
As Black people, we are loved for what we produce: sports, culture, style, and the arts,
but our bodies are not valued like those of our White counterparts.
Since the beginning of slavery, there's always been tension between Black and White women.
We've been at the mercy of their anger and not considered fully human.
But somehow she was human enough to nurse White babies at her Black breast.
She was human enough to be the belly warmer of the White slave owner at his request.
I know the tension plays out even every day at school and I know it's a drag.
Let's go talk to Karen with all your lips, cheekbones, curves, and swag.

Keisha:
Ms. Karen, just because I have something you don't does not require you to be mean.
Your demeaning phrases and your lunchroom gossip render me a victim at a murder scene.
I wear the bullet holes as an outfit from your words and dirty looks.
You made me feel like I'm easy; you broke me and now I'm shook.
Well, that's all it took to make me cry and believe the system is corrupt.
And sending me to the office is the body bag to cover me up.
But even if you give me sweatpants, these hips will still poke out.
My silhouette is no shadow but is like refreshing water in a drought.
My humanity is still present in any piece of fashion I wear.
My accent, sweet scent, and luscious textured crown will always be there.
I will not be afraid and I will not be ashamed.
No matter how many times you try to kill me, I will remain the same.
I still stand, I still grow, and I still learn to love you.
I will always have a nurturing heart, the same as all Black women do.

Mom:
You see, Karen, your name represents someone who uses whiteness for control.
But reconciliation should be your ultimate goal.
You're 80% of the schoolhouse, but not everyone's like you.
You need to watch the good ones and follow what they do.
My daughter's name is Keisha, an American name meaning "her life."
Today is when the torture ends, because I'm removing your knife.
You've caused tears to flow and hearts to hurt and ruined self-esteem.
You must hate yourself treating a child, yes, a child so cruel and so mean.
You don't belong in the schoolhouse; let the others do the job.
Because every time you speak, you cause my Keisha to sob.
I'm her mom, and I'll do whatever it takes to make sure you're gone.
Because no one deserves the way you've acted and carried on for so long.

> Your reign is over and it's time for healing and reconciliation.
> Get with the program now, baby, or hand in your resignation.
> I'll say it again like I said it before.
> Her life, my Keisha, and Karen, we ain't doing this no more!

It is very unlikely that this conversation would ever happen in real life because of the consequences that would follow. Children, specifically Black children, are taught to respect authority even when authority doesn't respect them. As a Black woman, it is easy to be characterized as the stereotypical angry Black woman, which is why many of us avoid these kinds of confrontations. This poem gave us the opportunity to be radical and to expose some of the tension between White teachers and Black girls in educational spaces. It allowed us to tell OUR story in OUR words by challenging stereotypes and creating a counter-narrative. So often, Black people, not wanting to "make waves," suffer silently. This poem allowed us to create space for our reality, thereby reclaiming our voice and power. We pray that those who identify with Mom and Keisha create space for these conversations to empower each other to confront racism. We pray that those who identify with Karen do better, because we reimagine a world where Black women and girls can experience the freedom they deserve.

Chapter 9

Conclusion

Whitneé Garrett-Walker

THE JOURNEY

Before deciding to become a school leader, I took my time. I watched the work of school leaders around me, who happened to be mostly Black and women, as they attempted to achieve a rhythm within their personal and professional lives. I was a witness while they endured and navigated the worst political scrimmages—from being reassigned in the middle of the school year to being pushed out of schools they had spent years redesigning, which led to the meticulous building of iron-clad walls around their hearts for protection. Through all of this, these Black women school leaders continued to show up for their school communities, but not for themselves. Looking back, I'm not sure that I felt that my experience of being a school leader would be different from theirs. Nonetheless, I was determined to live a life I could be proud of. For me, this looked like continuing to dance, read, spend time with my family, and travel. Throughout my journey, I was able to maintain some of the things I loved, but not everything. I was forced to choose, and this is not something I wanted to do, nor was I prepared to do it.

Every day of my first year as a school leader, my integrity felt compromised. I felt that I had to choose between my integrity and if I wanted, or at times needed, to engage in shady politics to get a request granted so as to best serve my students. There are definitely moments that I am not proud of—times when I towed the party line, stayed silent because a request was being granted. This experience of *choosing* was present every day and often left me and my position in the school in a state of purgatory. It felt like I was wading in a swamp of negativity. It became impossible to lead my teams and provide the resources they needed in order to serve without bending to the whims of district administrators and their ulterior political motives.

After my first year as an assistant principal at a large comprehensive high school, I witnessed our two women principals, one Filipina and the other White, being disrespectfully pushed out and replaced after they had been aggressively recruited. After witnessing this and how new principals had been selected before they went through the community-agreed-upon interview process, I stopped toeing the party line. I knew I was playing a risky game, but I did not care. I figured that the people who make up district leadership are capable of doing whatever they want. So instead of toeing the party line, I decided to walk in my truth and authenticity. I refused to accept vague answers to impactful, often one-sided decisions made in our school, like master schedule and funding structures. I understood that these massive systems that demonstrate a school's values and these decisions are a chance to be highly collaborative with our teacher-leaders. For example, we had been told for years that we had no funding for essentials like toilet paper. But we now had funding for co-principal salaries of more than half a million dollars? Of course I understood how budgets worked—there are discretionary funds, ADA, and various budgetary factors—but I also could not believe the intentional lack of prioritization of funding for programs that directly impacted youth. Because of this, I made the choice to stand in my truth and in solidarity with students and teachers by asking questions and being vocal about inequities I witnessed, such as those regarding suspensions and expulsions. The consequence: I was slowly relieved of the innovative projects that excited me and caused direct impact on our teachers and staff. Sizable grants that I had authored on behalf of our teachers were taken from me. Teams with whom I had worked hard to create sustainable community-based systems and structures were infiltrated with agendas and facilitators that did not include me. I was invited to the table as a thought partner with the organizations I had formed relationships with, only to be drained of my ideas, energy, and spirit for my projects. These new principals could not hold these meetings without me because of my institutional knowledge and relationships, and they knew this. However, during these meetings they made sure I was uncomfortable, that I was clear about who was in power, and that it was neither me nor the community organizations. I had never experienced being pushed out, and it was so incredibly passive-aggressive and insidious that when I brought it up to colleagues, I was made to feel as though I was going mad: "Whitneé, I didn't see this. I think you're too emotional." I was so embarrassed. I had never been put in this position before. I was angry, hurt, and felt deeply disrespected.

Over time, I hated coming to work. In fact, as I drove up the hill to school every day, I cried. I turned to my music—often N.W.A, Incubus, Célia Cruz, or Beyoncé's *Lemonade* album—to hold on to my reason for coming to work and not turn around and quit each day. I would park in my spot, put on my lipstick, fix my mascara, and be prepared to greet students as I walked to my office. It was painful. I had gotten into this routine for more than a year and I was breaking, slowly. My teachers and staff could tell I was unhappy, but I was their buffer, protecting them from the many changes coming down without community engagement. Because they knew this, they did all they could to make my load lighter. My students hugged me tighter and tighter each day. I never told my teams everything I was going through because I did not have to; they witnessed it. They often learned of responsibilities I had been stripped from when I did—in whole staff meetings or via email.

In January 2019 I started creating boundaries—leaving at 4:00 p.m., not working on weekends. They didn't know it, but my wife and I were preparing to expand our family. It was a very stressful time at work, and my co-principals continued to violate these boundaries. My blood pressure was consistently high, I was having frequent panic attacks, and I had no healthy coping skills. One morning I woke up and bled, immensely. It took a week and blood tests to find out that I had miscarried. I had lost my first baby after a week from hell, which included being forced to physically restrain students and take on even more time-sensitive tasks outside of my responsibilities. Even after I told these new principals about my miscarriage, I felt myself grow cold and shameful because I didn't feel safe or that I could be vulnerable with them. I remember one of them wanting to physically express concern through a hug, and even though I wasn't comfortable being touched, I allowed it. I thought that she understood and would potentially change her behavior because she "empathized" with me in this moment. I understand now that there was no way they could have seen me as a whole person who is worthy of respect, empathy, or understanding. My expectations for humanity were too high.

My 2019 spring semester was a rough one for so many reasons. During the annual retreat with my academy, hosted in my home, we heard on the news that teachers were officially going on strike. We stood around my kitchen and I told them, "I stand in solidarity with you. I know you love our kids. Just know that I love them just as much. All I ask is that you not make this an 'us against them' moment, because I will be on the line with you every day." Not only was I mourning a loss, but I also lived and worked through my first teacher strike. My nerves were shot every day as teachers who were not members of my team exhibited a lack of criticality and care toward students, me, one another, and, at times, toward substitutes who had no choice but to cross the line and work. As we came back together after the strike, our school morale was positively shattered. There was no trust, care, or willingness to engage in response to the ugliness we had witnessed as a school. Instead of tackling this for 250 staff members, I brought my 70-person staff together to begin our healing. We were determined to restore any faith that had been lost.

Because the Indigenous practice of restorative justice is a foundational tool used in our community agreements and overall function, this process went relatively smoothly. I listened to my staff, but I was clear about my refusal to take on additional emotional labor or responsibility for things outside my control. We came back to one another over time.

After a couple of procedures, in May I became pregnant; I told no one. I made the decision to not work in the summer. I took the time to re-ground myself in my new reality of motherhood. I was terrified and determined not to lose this baby. I took the summer to enjoy being with my family, travel, and feel my baby grow. When I returned to work in August, it was the start of the 2019–2020 school year and I was 12 weeks pregnant.

THE INCIDENT

The beginning of this 2019–2020 school year was tough; it was the most volatile in all my years in education. There were multiple fights happening daily for the first seven weeks of school. Even with back-to-back meetings with families, restorative and peacekeeping circles, and all the preventive methods and relationship building, a lot of different types of assaults continued to occur. Our administrative team was getting hit hard. By this time, I had already had some very intense meetings with families where I had been threatened by parents. On one occasion I had been threatened and verbally assaulted by a Black father who told me that "I should watch my back." He knew I was pregnant, but he was angry with me because I had to refer his child for expulsion due to proven sexual harassment. I asked to be taken off the case and for a stay-away order because he had threatened me. I was told I had to complete the paperwork for the case and that no stay-away order could be given. This is yet another time when I felt unsafe and unsupported.

I woke up on Tuesday, September 24, 2019, a healthy 21 weeks pregnant and ready for the day. I remember what I was wearing—a yellow shirt, really cute green maternity pants, and my Chuck Taylor sneakers. I remember this day perfectly because I was especially excited that my baby bump had begun to grow more pronounced. I had also started to feel my baby kick more intensely the previous weekend, and it was a joy I had never known.

During lunchtime, one of the principals removed security from the front gate, and three young Black girls (who were not our students) were able to walk onto our campus and physically assault one of our students. They caused a huge stir and an unbreakable mob of hundreds of students who witnessed this altercation. This ended up turning into a 1:1 fight. There were several high-pitched radio calls for "all hands on deck," and I felt conflicted about stepping outside my office to help because of the nature of the incident taking place. I was asked to stay with our student who had been assaulted, who was visibly escalated and screaming at the top of her lungs. At this point, her upset mother and sister were on the way, and I felt very anxious because I knew I was going to have to step in as I normally would to deal with this. I wasn't the only pregnant woman in this room—there was another pregnant support staff member there—and we were both feeling really uncomfortable. But what else could we do?

Once our student's mother arrived, I was radioed and walked the student to the front of the school. As we began to walk towards the car, our student started to get upset all over again, which she had every right to do. All of a sudden, the student's sister, a former student, started popping off, which she also had every right to do. Our student's safety had been compromised because the school did not have security at the front gate. Here I am, a Black mother and administrator, standing in front of this Black family and trying to help them. For a while we were on the same page, and all I wanted to do was get them safely off campus. I could feel the situation escalating, as the police had just arrived to the school. In a matter of seconds, I went from being helpful to this Black family to being cursed out and made the enemy. This did not faze me; I kept walking and telling the student's mother, "I completely understand how you feel, but I can't take you in the office for safety reasons. Let's get you and your children off campus." After nearly a decade of working in this school district, I knew angry parents and police could result in situations even more terrible than the initial incident. After being cursed out for a while by the mother, I turned to her and said, "I'm trying to help you and your child. You can't even see that, but you won't call me a bitch again. It is unprofessional, disrespectful, and not okay. Help me help you." I was tired of being disrespected and called *out of my name*. I understood her anger. It was warranted, of course. As school administrators, we learn to take these verbal body shots daily, without space to stand up for ourselves or our humanity.

Before I knew it, the two daughters dashed over to one of the entrances to the administrative building, where the other Black girls were being handcuffed by school police. I walked over and put my arm in the front of them. "You see I'm pregnant. Relax. It's fine. Step back. Think about this." The mom came over and said, "Move, bitch," and pushed me in the stomach. I fell. After a few moments, I got up and walked over to a tree in front of my office. I couldn't breathe. I put my hand on the tree to catch my breath. I have believed my entire life that I have mild anxiety. But this was something I'd never experienced. I was navigating two different identities, one as a Black woman school leader and the other as a new mother, and I was doing this in real time. For the first and last time, I put my role as a Black woman school leader before that of being a mother and was injured deeply—not just physically but psychologically. I felt it immediately.

At that point, one of the new co-principals told a Black male teacher to come and walk me to his empty classroom. I could barely walk. I could barely breathe. I was having a severe panic attack, and our school nurse, a Black woman, was called. The other administrators and the nurse wanted to call an ambulance because I was shaking violently and struggling to walk. I struggled to catch my breath, and my blood pressure had skyrocketed. I just told them to call my wife, "She'll be here in 20 minutes. Just call her." All I could do was hold my stomach and sob. I was cracked completely open.

When my wife arrived, we went straight to the emergency room. We got a full ultrasound. There was our baby, completely fine, doing flips and relaxing. In that moment, when I heard my baby's heartbeat and we saw they were healthy, all of the adrenaline rushed from my body and an unimaginable pain took over. My back felt twisted and bunched. The left side of my stomach had begun to bruise with shades of purple and green. In the emergency room, my obstetrician, a Black woman, came to see me. She took me off work immediately. When filling out emergency room paperwork and writing that it was a workplace incident, I felt shame. I kept thinking to myself, *I should be able to dust off and keep going*, but I couldn't. Not this time. This was the first time I had experienced high blood pressure during my pregnancy, and it continued throughout the rest of my pregnancy. The impact of this event caused me to be induced instead of going into labor naturally due to concerns of preeclampsia.

CRACKED IN HALF

On Friday, September 27, three days after the incident, I got a voicemail from my grandmother and a text from a family friend saying, "I'm so sorry for your loss." I called my grandmother, and she was in tears. My grandfather had passed away while I was in the doctor's office. If it were possible to be completely cracked in half, that is what I felt. I was undone. I think I had expected my co-principals to have at least an ounce of care and compassion, but I got nothing. As one could imagine, sending an email to request bereavement leave was tough. I didn't even get the standard response of "I'm sorry for your loss." Instead, they had postponed things that I held, like emergency drills, and shared with the staff: "Ms. G. W. had a death in the family, and we will wait until she returns to do the drills." While this may not seem like a harmful response, consider my privacy; I was not asked if this information could be shared. It should also be considered that I had sent an email from my hospital bed to my administrator team delineating the flow of the emergency drills; now, days later, everything still had to be held by me, a Black woman who had just been assaulted while pregnant and had just lost her grandfather. I was not shown an ounce of humanity. I had given all I had to this campus, and the fact that I received so little when I needed to be shown care shattered me. No one from the administrator team offered condolences or asked me if I was okay. It took me two weeks to build the courage to be honest enough to share how I felt. I sent an email sharing with the administrator team that I felt the lack of execution of the emergency drills was blamed on me and my absence. I also shared that I'd sent an email from a hospital bed with clear steps on how to execute the emergency drills. In response to my email, I was told by one of my co-principals that I was unprofessional and to call her immediately. I began to have another panic attack, so I had no choice but to let it go. I stopped checking my email for weeks, except communication about workers' compensation with the district. It was so difficult to talk with people during this time. I could barely talk to people about this incident without having panic attacks. My wife had to help me check and respond to emails. She had to help me have conversations because I was nervous, on edge, scared, ashamed, and angry all the time. This was not healthy for me or my baby. I finally reached out to my obstetrician and told her, "I need to talk to somebody. I can't do this anymore and I need help, now."

She referred me to a psychiatrist, and, honestly, I considered not going. I had so many feelings, and I was scared to share them. I didn't want to be seen as an unfit person or mother, which is a reality for many Black birthing people experiencing mental health concerns. Despite my negative feelings, I was pleasantly shocked by how easy it was to tell the doctor how I felt about what happened to me and had no skills to cope with. He said, "When you break your arm, you get immediate care. For you, you're not broken. You've got to start healing, but you need space to do it." During my second visit, I was formally diagnosed with PTSD and anxiety. I immediately began crying. I asked, "How am I supposed to heal through this? I can't work and heal, not yet. Not right now. I'm so scared of what would happen to me and what would happen to my baby." I was immediately taken off work until my maternity leave began, and the next day I started group therapy.

I wasn't particularly excited about going to therapy, but I was at the point where something had to give. I went to group therapy first. My first meeting, I was in a room full of strangers at Kaiser with two male therapists of color, and the first topic was self-compassion. This is when I learned that I gave all my compassion to my work and none to myself. I blamed myself for being assaulted and felt shame because of the workload left for my peers. This was a red flag that I clearly needed the space to re-center my priorities, as well as heal through my current reality.

SEEKING HEALING

This incident attempted to steal the joy of my pregnancy and love for my research away from me. I wouldn't let it. I dove back into data collection for my dissertation (Garrett-Walker, 2021) and used the time to listen to the life and work experiences of current and retired Black women school leaders in my district. I never told my participants what happened to me. I just sat there and enjoyed sharing space with them. They didn't know it, but they were the glue that held me together. Hearing their stories made me think about the ways I continue to show up for myself *and* my school community. As I asked my participants the questions "What keeps you here?" "What brings you joy?" "Why do you do this?" "Why do you stay?" I also reflected on these same questions and wrote in my fieldwork notebook out of curiosity for my own answers. I wrote, "I stay because of kids. Who else is going to support, and protect, and love, and cherish students who have been historically and multiply-marginalized at my school? Who else can I trust to interrupt racist teaching for them? I'm the only administrator who is willing to do this at my school."

I'M AWAKE NOW

I have learned that healing is not linear. Healing is necessary and ongoing. I still have nightmares. I still cry. Even though I look at my beautiful 14-month-old baby and am so enamored with them, I also think about how they could have died because of how hard I fell. But they didn't. Every time they smile at me, it's a reminder that I'm here. I'm not broken. I am whole. I make the decision every single day to heal. Every day, I do the work of reframing the way I think about myself, the way I perceive the world and my place in it. After having my baby in February 2020, I realized that my focus, the way I approached and understood my research and my work as a practitioner, was different. I too have moments of resistance. I exhibit critical hope, and I am actively on a journey of radical healing.

IT'S OKAY TO BE A WILD SEED: A LOVE LETTER TO NEW BLACK WOMEN SCHOOL LEADERS

Dear Sis,
    I call you Sis because, while we've never met, you're reading a personal chapter of my life intended for you. This piece of writing might be the rawest

offering I will ever give to the world, and since I'm already raw, I might as well keep it real with you.

I want to speak to your spirit, the fighter in you. The resistance in you. The wild seed planted by our ancestors. I want you to know that it's okay to be a wild seed. Be unapologetic. Be free. *And* know that you will pay a price for this. But you'll also pay a larger internal price for sitting on your hands instead of doing what you know is right for kids, your staff, and, don't forget, what's right for you. I know that your preparation program will most likely not talk about how Black women lead. Leadership is like breath for us. It's what we do, *and* how we survive.

I want to shift this narrative for you right now. We know how to lead, *and* we know how to rest. We know what feels right and what doesn't. We know how to heal. Since no one is going to give you permission to rest, I will. Please rest. The evenings and weekends are meant for you to decompress, slow your mind, and be with yourself and loved ones. Yes, answering emails late at night might lighten your load for the next morning, but let's be real—it really doesn't. You get no points for burning out. Since no one will give you permission to do what feels right, I will. There are spaces where we are welcomed (as welcoming as folx can be toward Black women), and you know what that feels like. There are spaces that are closed to us, and you definitely know what that feels like. You do not have to compromise your integrity to lead effectively and intentionally. You do not have to compromise your purpose to lead sustainably. When something does not feel right, more than likely, it isn't. Follow your intuition.

Before you take the plunge into the work of becoming a school leader, I want you to make a list detailing the qualities of who you are. I want you to keep this in your office for the days when you feel lost, compromised, or like you don't matter. I want you to look at how you named and defined yourself. No one has this power but you.

I'm not going to give you tips on how to navigate politics or engage in decision-making—you already know how to do this; otherwise you wouldn't be considering leading a school. What I will share is what my Momzie says: "Just listen. People will tell on themselves and share their true intentions." My hope for you is to stay free and grounded. Continue with a routine that allows you to care for your mind, body, spirit, and ability to connect, because this work will attempt to break you.

Much love and respect,
Whitneé

THE MAJESTIC PLACE

Whitneé L. Garrett-Walker

I see you, as I see myself.

Whole

I feel you,
   Tender.
You are owed much, my love.
   How my heart aches for you to be as free as me.
If you were to describe what it is to be free, what might you say?
Who might you tell? How would you get there? Where is it?
   You might tell us about the sunflowers and how they all faced the sun.
      You might see your grandmother sitting on a porch sharing her sweet tea with her sweet pea.
   You might tell everyone you knew that Moses was coming and it was time.
   You would boat, run, crawl, scream, cry—to get Free.
The Majestic Place is in your reach.
Just close your eyes
And breathe deep
And, again, Breathe.
Your breath is your body reminding your spirit of its existence on Earth.

Freedom begins with our breath.

   Then our minds.

When was the last time you freed your mind and let the rest follow?

When was the last time you took your time?

Freedom is a choice, a choice we make daily.

The Majestic Place is both location and feeling.

It is breath. It is laughter. It is rest. It is warmth. It is (re)membering. It is connection. It is grounding. It is health. It is sustenance. It is fruit. It is the Future. It is Now.

References

PART I: MOTHER'S MILK INTRODUCTION

Collins, P. H. (1991). The meaning of motherhood in Black culture and Black mother-daughter relationships. In Patricia Bell-Scott et al. (Eds.), *Double stitch: Black women write about mothers and daughters* (pp. 42–60). HarperCollins.

Cruz-Janzen, M. I. (2001). Latinegras: Desired women: Undesirable mothers, daughters, sisters, and wives. *Frontiers (Boulder), 22*(3), 168–183. https://doi.org/10.1353/fro.2001.0035

Edghill-Walden, V., Boston, T., & Palmer, A. (2018). We speak their names: Counter-narratives of Black women liberators. *Black History Bulletin, 81*(1), 5–14. https://doi.org/10.1353/bhb.2018.0005

Grady-Hunt, A. A. (2021). Black mothering as spiritual praxis: Engendering a multi-generational leadership paradigm. *Review and Expositor (Berne), 118*(3), 358–366. https://doi.org/10.1177/00346373211070628

Sakho, J. R. (2017). Black activist mothering: Teach me about what teaches you. *Western Journal of Black Studies, 41*(1/2), 6–19.

CHAPTER 2: *DANDO LECHE*

Abdullah, M. (2012). Womanist mothering: Loving and raising the revolution. *Western Journal of Black Studies, 36*(1), 57–67.

Alexander, T. (2010). Roots of leadership: Analysis of the narratives from African American women leaders in higher education. *International Journal of Learning, 17*(4), 193–204. https://doi.org/10.18848/1447-9494/cgp/v17i04/46973

Anaya, R. (2011). Graduate student mothers of color: The intersectionality between graduate student, motherhood, and women of color in higher education. *Intersections: Women's and Gender Studies in Review Across Disciplines* (9).

Bass, L. (2012). When care trumps justice: The operationalization of Black feminist caring in educational leadership. *International Journal of Qualitative Studies in Education, 25*(1), 73–87. https://doi.org/10.1080/09518398.2011.647721

Blackmer Reyes, K., & Curry Rodríguez, J. E. (2012). Testimonio: Origins, terms, and resources. *Equity & Excellence in Education, 45*(3), 525–538. https://doi.org/10.1080/10665684.2012.698571

Byrne-Jiménez, M., & García, W. (2021). Un cafecito. In M. A. Martinez & S. Méndez-Morse (Eds.), *Latinas Leading Schools*. Information Age Publishing.

Caballero, C., et al. (2019). *The Chicana motherwork anthology*. University of Arizona Press.

Castagno, A. E. (2021). From professional development to native nation building: Opening up space for leadership, relationality, and self-determination through the Diné Institute for Navajo Nation Educators. *Educational Studies, 57*(3), 322–334. https://doi.org/10.1080/00131946.2021.1892686

Cortes, K. L. (2019). Between Blackness and Africanness: Indexing Puerto Rican identity through discourse in Northern California. In M. K. Clark, P. W. Mnyandu, & L. Azalia (Eds.), *Pan African spaces: Essays on Black transnationalism*. Lexington Books.

Cortes, K. L. (2020). AfroBoriqua mothering: Teaching/learning Blackness in a Bay Area AfroPuerto Rican community of practice. *Journal of Cultural and Ethnic Studies, 7*(2), 127–146. https://doi.org/10.29333/ejecs/351

Crenshaw, K. (1991). Mapping the margins: Identity politics, intersectionality, and violence against women. *Stanford Law Review, 43*(6), 1241–1299.

Darder, A. (2017). *Reinventing Paulo Freire: A pedagogy of love* (2nd ed.). Routledge.

Dei, G. J. S. (2000). Rethinking the role of Indigenous knowledges in the academy. *International Journal of Inclusive Education, 4*(2), 111–132. https://doi.org/10.1080/136031100284849

Dei, G. J. S. (2017). *Reframing blackness and Black solidarities through anti-colonial and decolonial prisms* (1st ed., vol. 4). Springer International Publishing AG. https://doi.org/10.1007/978-3-319-53079-6

Delgado Bernal, D., Burciaga, R., & Flores Carmona, J. (2012). Chicana/Latina testimonios: Mapping the methodological, pedagogical, and political. *Equity & Excellence in Education, 45*(3), 363–372. https://doi.org/10.1080/10665684.2012.698149

DeNicolo, C. P., & Gónzalez, M. (2015). Testimoniando en Nepantla: Using testimonio as a pedagogical tool for exploring embodied literacies and bilingualism. *Journal of Language and Literacy Education, 11*(1), 109–126.

Dewi Oka, C. (2016). Mothering as revolutionary praxis. In *Revolutionary mothering: Love on the front lines* (pp. 51–57). PM Press.

Duran, V. (2019). MALA: Mama academic liberadora activista. In C. Caballero et al. (Eds.), *The Chicana Motherwork Anthology: Porque sin madres no hay revolución*. University of Arizona Press.

Ebaugh, H. R., & Curry, M. (2000). Fictive kin as social capital in new immigrant communities. *Sociological Perspectives, 43*(2), 189–209. https://doi.org/10.2307/1389793

Elenes, C. (2013). Nepantla, spiritual activism, new tribalism: Chicana feminist transformative pedagogies and social justice education. *Journal of Latino/Latin American Studies, 5*(3), 132–141. https://doi.org/10.18085/llas.5.3.w3528w365m860188

Figueroa, Y. C. (2020). Your lips: Mapping Afro-Boricua feminist becomings. *Frontiers: A Journal of Women Studies, 41*(1), 1–11. https://doi.org/10.1353/fro.2020.a755337

Fleetwood, N. (2011). *Troubling vision: Performance, visuality, and Blackness*. The University of Chicago Press.

Garcia, W. (2018). The intersectionality of Afro-Latinx school leaders: A qualitative inquiry. (Publication No. 13863930) [Doctoral dissertation, Michigan State University]. ProQuest Dissertations & Theses Global (2235423543). https://www.proquest.com/dissertations-theses/africana-women-stories-mothering-african-centered/docview/2235423543/se-2

García-Louis, C., & Cortes, K. L. (2020). Rejecting Black and rejected back: AfroLatinx college students' experiences with anti-AfroLatinidad. *Journal of Latinos and Education*. https://doi.org/10.1080/15348431.2020.1731692

García-Louis, C., & Reyes-Barriéntez, A. (2022). Maternidad fronteriza amidst COVID-19 pandemic: Testimonios of Mami scholars' resistance. *Journal of Women and Gender in Higher Education, 15*(1), 1–20. https://doi.org/10.1080/26379112.2022.2026368

Garcia Peña, L. (2022). *Translating Blackness: Latinx colonialities in global perspective*. Duke University Press. https://doi.org/10.1515/9781478023289

Godreau, I. P. (2015). *Scripts of Blackness: Race, cultural nationalism, and US colonialism in Puerto Rico*. University of Illinois Press.

Gorman, A. (2021). *Call us what we carry: Poems*. Penguin Random House.

Grant, C. M. (2012). Advancing our legacy: A Black feminist perspective on the significance of mentoring for African-American women in educational leadership. *International Journal of Qualitative Studies in Education, 25*(1), 101–117. https://doi.org/10.1080/09518398.2011.647719

Greene Brown, T. (2020). *Parenting for liberation: A guide for raising Black children*. Feminist Press.

Gumbs, A. P. (2016). M/other ourselves: A Black queer feminist genealogy for radical mothering. In A. P. Gumbs, C. Martens, & M. Williams (Eds.), *Revolutionary mothering: Love on the front lines*. PM Press.

hooks, b. (1994). *Feminist theory: From margin to center*. South End Press.

hooks, b. (2014). *Teaching to transgress*. Routledge.

Horsford, S. D. (2012). This bridge called my leadership: An essay on Black women as bridge leaders in education. *International Journal of Qualitative Studies in Education, 25*(1), 11–22. https://doi.org/10.1080/09518398.2011.647726

Horsford, S. D., & Tillman, L. (2012). Inventing herself: Examining the intersectional identities and educational leadership of Black women in the USA. *International Journal of Qualitative Studies in Education, 25*(1), 1–9. https://doi.org/10.1080/09518398.2011.647727

Hoy, V. C. (2010). Negotiating among invisibilities. In M. Jimènez Román & J. Flores (Eds.), *The Afro-Latin@ reader: History and culture in the United States*. Duke University Press.

Jorge, A. (2010). The Black Puerto Rican woman in contemporary American society. In M. Jimènez Román and J. Flores (Eds.), *The Afro-Latin@ reader: History and culture in the United States*. Duke University Press.

Kenny, C. (2012). Liberating leadership theory. In *Living Indigenous Leadership: Native Narratives on Building Strong Communities* (pp. 1–14). University of British Columbia Press. https://doi.org/10.59962/9780774823487-003

Laó-Montes, A. (2005). Afro-Latinidades and the diasporic imaginary. *Iberoamericana (Madrid, Spain), 5*(17), 117–130.

Laó-Montes, A. (2007). Decolonial moves: Trans-locating African diaspora spaces. *Cultural Studies, 21*(2–3), 309–338. https://doi.org/10.1080/09502380601164361

Lara, A. M. (2012). Bodies and memories: Afro-Latina identities in motion. In M. Moreno Vega, M. Alba, & Y. Modestin (Eds.), *Women warriors of the AfroLatina diaspora*. Arte Público Press.

Lara, I. (2005). Bruja positionalities: Toward a Chicana/Latina spiritual activism. *Chicana/Latina Studies, 4*(2), 10–45.

Laurent-Perrault, E. (2012). A life spirals: Journeys of an Afro-Latina activist. In M. Moreno Vega, M. Alba, and Y. Modestin (Eds.), *Women warriors of the Afro-Latina diaspora*. Arte Público Press.

Lopez Oro, P. J. (2020). Garifunizando ambas Américas: Hemispheric entanglements of Blackness/Indigeneity/AfroLatinidad. *Postmodern Culture, 31*(1). https://doi.org/10.1353/PMC.2020.0025

Lugones, M. (2010). Toward a decolonial feminism. *Hypatia, 25*(4), 742–759. https://doi.org/10.1111/j.1527-2001.2010.01137.x

Matias, C. (2011). "Cheryl Matias, PhD and mother of twins": Counter storytelling to critically analyze how I navigated the academic application, negotiation, and relocation process [paper presentation]. American Educational Research Association Annual Meeting. New Orleans.

Matias, C. E., & Liou, D. D. (2015). Tending to the heart of communities of color: Towards critical race teacher activism. *Urban Education, 50*(5), 601–625. https://doi.org/10.1177/0042085913519338

Medina, L., & Gonzales, M. R. (Eds.). (2019). *Voices from the ancestors: Xicanx and Latinx spiritual expressions and healing practices*. University of Arizona Press.

Modestin, Y. (2012). The whispers of the ancestors: Development of a Black, proud, Panamanian voice. In M. Moreno Vega, M. Alba, & Y. Modestin (Eds.), *Women warriors of the Afro-Latina diaspora*. Arte Público Press.

Moraga C. (1981). Theories in the flesh. In C. Moraga & G. Anzaldúa (Eds.), *This bridge called my back: Writings by radical women of color*. Persephone Press.

Ospina, S., & Foldy, E. (2009). A critical review of race and ethnicity in the leadership literature: Surfacing context, power and the collective dimensions of leadership. *The Leadership Quarterly, 20*(6), 876–896. https://doi.org/10.1016/j.leaqua.2009.09.005

Paris, D., & Winn, M. T. (2014). Preface: To humanize research. In *Humanizing research. Decolonizing qualitative inquiry with youth and communities* (pp. xiii–xxii). SAGE Publications.

Pérez Huber, L. (2009). Disrupting apartheid of knowledge: Testimonios as methodology in Latina/o critical race research in education. *International Journal of Qualitative Studies in Education, 22*(6), 639–654. https://doi.org/10.1080/09518390903333863

Plácido, S. (2017). Expanding the dialogues: Afro-Latinx feminisms. *Latinx Talk*, 28.

Radford-Hill, S. (1986). Considering feminism as a model for social change. In *Feminist studies/critical studies* (pp. 157–172). Palgrave Macmillan.

Rivera-Rideau, P. R. (2017). Expanding the dialogues: Afro-Latinx feminisms. *Latinx Talk*, 28.

Segura, D. A., & Facio, E. (2008). Adelante mujer: Latina activism, feminism, and empowerment. In *Latinas/os in the United States: Changing the face of América* (pp. 23–38). Springer.

Smith, L. T., Tuck, E., & Yang, K. W. (Eds.). (2018). *Indigenous and decolonizing studies in education*. Routledge.

Urrieta, L. (2007). Figured worlds and education: An introduction to the special issue. *The Urban Review, 39*(2), 107–116. https://doi.org/10.1007/s11256-007-0051-0

Wirtz, K. (2007). How diasporic religious communities remember: Learning to speak the "tongue of the Oricha" in Cuban santería. *American Ethnologist, 34*(1), 108–126. https://doi.org/10.1525/ae.2007.34.1.108

York-Barr, J., & Duke, K. (2004). What do we know about teacher leadership? Findings from two decades of scholarship. *Review of Educational Research, 74*(3), 255–316. https://doi.org/10.3102/00346543074003255

Zamora, O. Z. (2017). Expanding the dialogues: Afro-Latinx feminisms. *Latinx Talk*, 28.

CHAPTER 3: BEYOND THE VEIL

Boylorn, R. M. (2008). As seen on TV: An autoethnographic reflection on race and reality television. *Critical Studies in Media Communication, 25*(4), 413–433. https://doi.org/10.1080/15295030802327758

Brewer, R. M. (1999). Theorizing race, class and gender: The new scholarship of Black feminist intellectuals and Black women's labor. *Race, Gender & Class, 6*(2), 29–47.

Chance, N. L. (2022). Resilient leadership: A phenomenological exploration into how Black women in higher education leadership navigate cultural adversity. *Journal of Humanistic Psychology, 62*(1), 44–78. https://doi.org/10.1177/00221678211003000

Clifton, L. (1993). Won't you celebrate with me. In *The Book of Light* (p. 25). Copper Canyon Press.

Collins, P. H. (1986). Learning from the outsider within: The sociological significance of Black feminist thought. *Social Problems, 33*(6), S14–S32. https://doi.org/10.1525/sp.1986.33.6.03a00020

Collins, P. H. (2000). *Black feminist thought knowledge, consciousness, and the politics of empowerment.* Routledge.

Crenshaw, K. (1989). Demarginalizing the intersection of race and sex: A Black feminist critique of antidiscrimination doctrine, feminist theory, and antiracist politics. *University of Chicago Legal Forum, 1988*(1), 139–167. https://chicagounbound.uchicago.edu/uclf/vol1989/iss1/8

Crenshaw, K. (1990). Mapping the margins: Intersectionality, identity politics, and violence against women of color. *Stanford Law Review,* 43, 1241.

Custer, D. (2014). Autoethnography as a transformative research method. *The Qualitative Report, 19*(37), 1–13. https://doi.org/10.46743/2160-3715/2014.1011

Cyr, D., Weiner, J., & Burton, L. (2021). "I want to speak to a White person": Daily microaggressions and resilient leadership. *Journal of Cases in Educational Leadership, 24*(4), 60–73. https://doi.org/10.1177/1555458921997527

Dickens, D. D., Womack, V. Y., & Dimes, T. (2019). Managing hypervisibility: An exploration of theory and research on identity shifting strategies in the workplace among Black women. *Journal of Vocational Behavior, 113,* 153–163.

Drake, H. [@HannahDrake628]. (2019, October 14). Fix it, Black girl. Fix us, Black girl. Nurse us, Black girl. Teach us, Black girl. Be the help, Black [Tweet]. Twitter. https://twitter.com/hannahdrake628/status/1183930976004694016

Ellis, C., Adams, T. E., & Bochner, A. P. (2011). Autoethnography: An overview. *Historical Social Research/Historische sozialforschung,* 273–290.

Ellis, C. S., & Bochner, A. P. (2006). Analyzing analytic autoethnography: An autopsy. *Journal of Contemporary Ethnography, 35*(4), 429–449. https://doi.org/10.1177/0891241606286979

Hall, J. C., Everett, J. E., & Hamilton-Mason, J. (2011). Black women talk about workplace stress and how they cope. *Journal of Black Studies, 43*(2), 207–226. https://doi.org/10.1177/0021934711413272

Hersey, T. (2023, January 25). Rest is resistance. The Nap Ministry. https://thenapministry.com

hooks, bell. (2021). *Communion: The female search for love.* Perennial.

Jackson II, R. L. (2002). Cultural contracts theory: Toward an understanding of identity negotiation. *Communication Quarterly, 50*(3), 359–367.

Jackson, S., & Harris, S. (2007). African American female college and university presidents: Experiences and perceptions of barriers to the presidency. *Journal of Women in Educational Leadership, 5*(2), 119–137.

Jean-Marie, G., Williams, V. A., & Sherman, S. L. (2009). Black women's leadership experiences: Examining the intersectionality of race and gender. *Advances in Developing Human Resources, 11*(5), 562–581. https://doi.org/10.1177/1523422309351836

Lamsam, T. T. (2014). A cultural contracts perspective: Examining American Indian identity negotiations in academia. *Journal of Cultural Diversity, 21*(1), 29–35.

Linnabery, E., Stuhlmacher, A. F., & Towler, A. (2014). From whence cometh their strength: Social support, coping, and well-being of Black women professionals. *Cultural Diversity and Ethnic Minority Psychology, 20*(4), 541.

McCluney, C. L., & Rabelo, V. C. (2019). Conditions of visibility: An intersectional examination of black women's belongingness and distinctiveness at work. *Journal of Vocational Behavior, 113*, 143–152. https://doi.org/10.1016/j.jvb.2018.09.008

McCluney, C. L., et al. (2021). To be, or not to be . . . Black: The effects of racial codeswitching on perceived professionalism in the workplace. *Journal of Experimental Social Psychology, 97*, 104–199. https://doi.org/10.1016/j.jesp.2021.104199

Parker, P. S. (2001). African American women executives' leadership communication within dominant-culture organizations: (Re)conceptualizing notions of collaboration and instrumentality. *Management Communication Quarterly, 15*(1), 42–82.

Rabelo, V. C., Robotham, K. J., & McCluney, C. L. (2021). "Against a sharp white background": How Black women experience the white gaze at work. *Gender, Work & Organization, 28*(5), 1840–1858.

Ronai, C. R. (1996). My mother is mentally retarded. In C. Ellis & A. P. Bochner (Eds.), *Composing ethnography: Alternative forms of qualitative writing* (pp. 109–131). AltaMira.

Rosser-Mims, D. (2010). Black feminism: An epistemological framework for exploring how race and gender impact black women's leadership development. *Advancing Women in Leadership, 30*. https://doi.org/10.21423/awlj-v30.a301

Shorter-Gooden, K. (2004). Multiple resistance strategies: How African American women cope with racism and sexism. *Journal of Black Psychology, 30*(3), 406–425. https://doi.org/10.1177/0095798404266050

Spry, T. (2001). Performing autoethnography: An embodied methodological praxis. *Qualitative Inquiry, 7*(6), 706–732. https://doi.org/10.1177/107780040100700605

Ting-Toomey, S. (2015). Identity negotiation theory. In J. Bennett (Ed.), *Sage encyclopedia of intercultural competence* (pp. 418–422). Sage Publishing.

CHAPTER 4: REFUELING

Asare, J. G. (2020, September 22). Misogynoir: The unique discrimination that Black women face. *Forbes.* https://www.forbes.com/sites/janicegassam/2020/09/22/misogynoir-the-unique-discrimination-that-black-women-face/?sh=6b17fe2356ef

Blackman-Richards, N. (2019, December 5). Personal email to vice-president of enrollment & student retention and vice-president of human resources.

Blackman-Richards, N. (2022, March 25). Personal email to college president & public safety leadership.

Blackman-Richards, N., Jimenez, J., & Pusey-Reid, E. (2023). Deconstructing standards of Whiteness to establish the power of Black women. In *The experiences of Black women diversity practitioners in historically White institutions*. IGI Global.

Blackman-Richards, N., et al. (2022, January 11). Public email to college president & dean of diversity.

Brooks, R. (2018). Looking to foremothers for strength: A brief biography of the colored woman's league. *Women's Studies, 47*(6), 609–616. https://doi.org/10.1080/00497878.2018.1492407

Chisholm, S. (1971). Race, revolution and women. *The Black Scholar, 3*(4), 17–21. http://www.jstor.org/stable/41203705

Coleman, M. A. (2008). *Making a way out of no way: A womanist theology*. Fortress Press.

Collins, P. H. (2000). *Black feminist thought: Knowledge, consciousness, and the politics of empowerment*. Routledge.

Crenshaw, K. (1989). Demarginalizing the intersection of race and sex: A Black feminist critique of anti-discrimination doctrine, feminist theory and anti-racist politics. *The University of Chicago Legal Forum, 140*, 139.

Curtis, S. (2017). Black women's intersectional complexities: The impact on leadership. *Management in Education, 31*(2), 94–102. https://doi.org/10.1177/0892020617696635

Curtis S. E. (2014). *Black women leaders in early years education* [PhD dissertation]. Leeds Beckett University.

Davis, V. (2022, September 16). *Viola Davis and Thuso Mbedu on physically preparing for "The Woman King" | Extended Interview*. Etalk. YouTube. https://youtu.be/MDZVDwlX1iE

Echavarria, E., & Williams, O. (2022). Heeding the signs: Using contemplative practice for sustainability as Black racial equity facilitators. *The Journal of Contemplative Inquiry, 9*(1), 149–162.

Ellis, L. (2020). For colleges, protests over racism may put everything on the line. *Chronicle of Higher Education*, 12. https://www.chronicle.com/article/for-colleges-protests-over-racism-may-put-everything-on-the-line

Evans, L., & Moore, W. L. (2015). Impossible burdens: White institutions, emotional labor, and micro-resistance. *Social Problems, 62*, 439–454.

Gates, H. L., et al. (2022, October 4). *Making Black America | Hosted by Prof. Henry Louis Gates Jr. | Episode 1* [Video]. PBS. YouTube. https://youtu.be/wfw2317bVIo

Grant, J. (2014, March 26). *Journey to liberation: The legacy of womanist theology* [Video] Union Theological Seminary. YouTube. https://youtu.be/PjhtUGqFCWg

hooks, b. (1994). *Love as the practice of freedom*. Outlaw Culture. Routledge.

Hunter, T., & Kelley, R. D. G. (2022, October 4). *Making Black America | Hosted by Prof. Henry Louis Gates Jr. | Episode 1* [Video]. PBS. YouTube. https://youtu.be/wfw2317bVIo

Kinser, A. E. (2010). *Motherhood and feminism: Seal studies*. Seal Press.

Lorde, A. (1982, February). "Learning from the 60's." Malcolm X Weekend. Harvard University. https://www.blackpast.org/african-american-history/1982-audre-lorde-learning-60s

Lorde, A. (1988). *A burst of light: And other essays*. Ixia Press.

Lorde, A. (2000). Poetry is not a luxury. *Making sense of women's lives: An introduction to women's studies* (p. 248). Routledge.

McCluney, C. L., & Rabelo, V. C. (2019). Conditions of visibility: An intersectional examination of Black women's belongingness and distinctiveness at work.

Journal of Vocational Behavior, 113, 143–152. https://doi.org/10.1016/j.jvb.2018.09.008

McEwen, B. S., & Stellar, E. (1993). Stress and the individual: Mechanisms leading to disease. *Archives of Internal Medicine (1960), 153*(18), 2093–2101. https://doi.org/10.1001/archinte.1993.00410180039004

Mgadmi, M. (2009). Black women's identity: Stereotypes, respectability and passionlessness (1890–1930). *Revue LISA/LISA E-journal, 7*(1), 40–55. https://doi.org/10.4000/lisa.806

Nyong'o, L. (2020, March 17). *Warrior women with Lupita Nyong'o (2019)*. Matheus Van der Berghe. YouTube. https://youtu.be/U7SNqXACAao

Olayiwola, P. (2022, October 4). *Making Black America | Hosted by Prof. Henry Louis Gates Jr. | Episode 1*. PBS. YouTube. https://youtu.be/wfw2317bVIo.

Pitchon, A. (2022). *Female warriors who led Africa*. History.com

Quaye, S. J., et al. (2019). Strategies for practicing self-care from racial battle fatigue. *Journal Committed to Social Change on Race and Ethnicity (JCSCORE), 5*(2), 95–131. https://www.jstor.org/stable/48645357

Smith, S. M. (2022). *Why radical self-care cannot wait: Strategies for Black women leaders NOW*. Perspectives on Urban Education (PennGSE).

Stevens, D. (writer). (2016). *The woman king* [screenplay]. TriStar Pictures.

Sue, D. W. (2010). *Microaggressions in everyday life: Race, gender & sexual orientation*. John Wiley & Sons, Inc.

Tan, M., et al. (2017). Neighborhood disadvantage and allostatic load in African American women at risk for obesity-related diseases. *Preventing Chronic Disease, 14*, 170143.

Townes, E. (2014, March 26). *Journey to liberation: The legacy of womanist theology* [Video] Union Theological Seminary. YouTube. https://youtu.be/PjhtUGqFCWg.

Walker, A. (2022). Black studies lecturer: "Boycotting *The woman king* makes no sense." *Michigan Chronicle*. Digital daily.

Williams, G. Y. (2008). *A passion for social equality: Mary McLeod Bethune's Race woman leadership and the New Deal*. University of Illinois at Chicago.

PART II: A WOMAN WILL MANIFEST INTRODUCTION

Figueroa, Y. C. (2020). Your lips: Mapping Afro-Boricua feminist becomings. *Frontiers: A Journal of Women Studies, 41*(1), 1–11.

Holder, A. M. B., Jackson, M. A., & Ponterotto, J. G. (2015). Racial microaggression experiences and coping strategies of Black women in corporate leadership. *Qualitative Psychology, 2*(2), 164–180. https://doi.org/10.1037/qup000002

Kinouani, G. (2022). *Living while Black: Using joy, beauty, and connection to heal racial trauma*. Beacon Press.

Lanier, D. A., Toson, S. J., & Walley-Jean, J. C. (2022). Black women leaders: Going high in a world of lows. *Advances in Developing Human Resources, 24*(3), 193–207.

Smith, E. B., & Nkomo, S. M. (2021). *Our separate ways, with a new preface and epilogue: Black and White women and the struggle for professional identity*. Harvard Business Press.

CHAPTER 5: LIFE, LOVE, AND LEADERSHIP

Andrews, M., Sclater, S., Squire, C., & Tamboukou, M. (2004). Narrative research. In *Qualitative Research Practice* (pp. 98–113). SAGE Publications. https://doi.org/10.4135/9781848608191

Ariemasuccess, LLC. (2022, August 30). *Amanda Seales on compliments*. [Video]. YouTube. https://youtube.com/shorts/w0isyFf4Dck?feature=shars

Armour, J. D. (2020). *N*gga theory: Race, language, unequal justice, and the law*. LARB Books.

Baptist, E. E. (2016). *The half has never been told: Slavery and the making of American capitalism*. Hachette UK.

Bell, E. L. J., & Nkomo, S. (2001). *Our separate ways: Black and white women and the struggle for professional identity*. Harvard Business School Press.

Brown, B. (2018). *Dare to lead: Brave work. Tough conversations. Whole hearts*. Random House.

Brown, B. (2021). *Atlas of the heart: Mapping meaningful connection and the language of human experience*. Random House.

Chase, S. E. (2003). Learning to listen: Narrative principles in a qualitative research methods course. In *Up close and personal: The teaching and learning of narrative research* (pp. 79–99). American Psychological Association. https://doi.org/10.1037/10486-005

Chinn, J. J., Martin, I. K., & Redmond, N. (2021). Health equity among Black women in the United States. *Journal of Women's Health, 30*(2), 212–219.

Cobb, F., & Krownapple, J. (2019). *Belonging through a culture of dignity: The keys to successful equity implementation*. Mimi & Todd Press.

Collins, P. H. (1998). *Fighting words: Black women and the search for justice*, vol. 7. University of Minnesota Press.

Crenshaw, K. (2013). Demarginalizing the intersection of race and sex: A Black feminist critique of antidiscrimination doctrine, feminist theory and antiracist politics. In *Feminist Legal Theories* (pp. 23–51). Routledge.

Dillard, C. (2021). *The spirit of our work: Black women teachers (re)member*. Beacon Press.

Fraser, H. (2004). Doing narrative research: Analyzing personal stories line by line. *Qualitative Social Work, 3*(2), 179–201.

References

Ginwright, S. A. (2022). *The four pivots: Reimagining justice, reimagining ourselves.* North Atlantic Books.

Hulse, C. (2022, March 24). The respectful Supreme Court hearing that wasn't. *New York Times.* https://www.nytimes.com/2022/03/24/us/politics/hostile-supreme-court-hearing-jackson.html

Jones, C., & Shorter-Gooden, K. (2003). *Shifting: The double lives of Black women in America.* HarperCollins.

Kaya, H. O. (2014). Revitalizing African indigenous ways of knowing and knowledge production. In M. Woons (Ed.), *Restoring indigenous self-determination* (p. 105). E-International Relations Publishing.

Kendi, I. X. (2016). *Stamped from the beginning: The definitive history of racist ideas in America.* Hachette UK.

Moody, A. T., & Lewis, J. A. (2019). Gendered racial microaggressions and traumatic stress symptoms among Black women. *Psychology of Women Quarterly, 43*(2), 201–214.

Muhammad, K. G. (2019). *The condemnation of Blackness: Race, crime, and the making of modern urban America, with a new preface.* Harvard University Press.

Mullen, C. A., & Robertson, K. (2014). *Shifting to fit: The politics of Black and White identity in school leadership.* IAP.

Ngara, C. (2007). African ways of knowing and pedagogy revisited. *Journal of Contemporary Issues in Education, 2*(2).

Okun, T., & Jones, K. (2000). White supremacy culture. *Dismantling racism: A workbook for social change groups*, Change Work. http://www.dismantlingracism.org/Dismantling_Racism/liNKs_files/whitesupcul09.pdf

Riessman, C. K. (1993). *Narrative analysis*, vol. 30. Sage.

Rogers-Ard, R. (2016). *The burden of admission: Profile of an African American female educational leader.* In T. E. Marsh & N. N. Croom (Eds.), *Envisioning a critical race praxis in K–12 education through counter-storytelling.* IAP.

Rogers-Ard, R., & Knaus, C. B. (2020). *Black educational leadership: From silencing to authenticity.* Routledge.

Safir, S., & Dugan, J. (2021). *Street data: A next-generation model for equity, pedagogy, and school transformation.* Corwin.

Sandelowski, M. (1991). Telling stories: Narrative approaches in qualitative research. *Image: The Journal of Nursing Scholarship, 23*(3), 161–166.

Schlein, C. (2020). Critical and narrative research perspectives on in-service intercultural teaching. *Theory into Practice, 59*(3), 321–331.

Taylor, S. R. (2021). *The body is not an apology: The power of radical self-love.* Berrett-Koehler Publishers.

Thompkins, T. (2005). *The real lives of strong Black women: Transcending myths, reclaiming joy.* Agate.

Wilkerson, I. (2020). The audacity, politics, and pragmatism of Black women's leadership. In *Caste: The origins of our discontents* (chapter 9). Random House.

CHAPTER 6: THE AUDACITY, POLITICS, AND PRAGMATISM OF BLACK WOMEN'S LEADERSHIP

Adedoyin, O. (2022, August 18). What happened to Black enrollment? *Chronicle of Higher Education.* https://www-chronicle-com.eu1.proxy.openathens.net/article/what-happened-to-black-enrollment

American Association of University Women. (n.d.). *Fast facts: Women of color in higher education.* https://www.aauw.org/resources/article/fast-facts-woc-higher-ed

American college president study 2017. (2017). American Council on Education. Washington, DC.

Bankole-Medina, K. (2021). A real-world discourse on intellectual identity, thought, leadership, and the Black Woman Academic Chair. *Palimpsest: A Journal on Women, Gender, and the Black International, 10*(2), 134–152.

Bass, L. (2009). Fostering an ethic of care in leadership: A conversation with five African American Women. *Advances in Developing Human Resources, 11*(5), 619–632.

Chance, N. L. (2021). The phenomenological inquiry into the influence of crucible experiences on the leadership development of Black women in higher education senior leadership. *Educational Management Administration & Leadership, 49*(4), 601–623.

Collins, P. H. (1986). Learning from the outsider within: The sociological significance of Black feminist thought. *Social Problems, 33*(6), 14–32.

Dictionary.com. (n.d.). Audacity. Retrieved June 14, 2024, from https://www.dictionary.com/browse/audacity

Dillard, C. B. (2016). To address suffering that the majority can't see: Lessons from Black women's leadership in the workplace. *New Directions for Adult and Continuing Education, 152*, 29–38.

Elder, C. C. (2022). *Power: The rise of Black Women in America.* Skyhorse Publishing.

Epps, S. K. (2008). African American women leaders in academic research libraries. *Libraries and the Academy, 8*(3), 255–272.

Gardner, L., Barrett, T. G., & Pearson, L. C. (2014). African American administrators at PWIs: Enablers of and barrios to career success. *Journal of Diversity in Higher Education, 7*(4), 235–251.

Gaudiano, P. (2019, December 19). Why Black women are better leaders. *Forbes.* https://www.forbes.com/sites/paologaudiano/2019/12/02/why-black-women-are-better-leaders/?sh=5b984dff259b

Holder, A. M. B., Jackson, M. A., & Ponterotto, J. G. (2015). Racial microaggression experiences and coping strategies of black women in corporate leadership. *Qualitative Psychology, 2*(2), 164–180.

Huang, B. L. (2017). Women of color advancing to senior leadership in U.S. academe. In H. Eggins (Ed.), *The changing role of women in higher education: Academic and leadership issues* (pp. 155–170). Springer.

Hughes, C. (2014). *American Black women and interpersonal leadership styles*. Sense Publishers.

Jackson, S., & Harris, S. (2007). African American female college and university presidents: Experiences and perceptions of barriers to the presidency. *Journal of Women in Educational Leadership, 5*(2), 119–137.

Kegan, R. (1982). *The evolving self: Problem and process in human development*. Harvard University Press.

Sales, S., Burke, M. G., & Cannonier, C. (2020). African American women leadership across contexts. Examining the internal traits and external factors on women leaders' perceptions of empowerment. *Journal of Management History, 26*(3), 353–376.

CHAPTER 7: THIS TOO SHALL PASS, OR WILL IT?

Ade-Serrano, Y. (2010). *Exploring the self-definition and individuality of Back professional women* [PhD dissertation, City University London]. City University Psychology Department. https://openaccess.city.ac.uk/id/eprint/8736

Burey, J-A. (2020, December 26). *Why you should not bring your authentic self to work*. TEDxSeattle. https://www.youtube.com/watch?v=HRi-jpzBiGo

Chartered Institute of Personnel and Development. (2021, 24 May). *Developing an anti-racism strategy*. https://www.cipd.co.uk/knowledge/fundamentals/relations/diversity/anti-racism-strategy#gref

Clance, P. R., & Imes, S. A. (1978). The imposter phenomenon in high achieving women: Dynamics and therapeutic intervention. *Psychotherapy: Theory, Research & Practice, 15*(3), 241–247. https://doi.org/10.1037/h0086006

Crenshaw, K. (1989). Demarginalizing the intersection of race and sex: A Black feminist critique of antidiscrimination doctrine, feminist theory and antiracist politics. *University of Chicago Legal Forum, 1*(8), 139–167. https://chicagounbound.uchicago.edu/uclf/vol1989/iss1/8

Crenshaw, K. (1991). Mapping the margins: Intersectionality, identity politics, and violence against women of color. *Stanford Law Review, 43*(6), 1241–1299. https://doi.org/10.2307/1229039

Dobbin, F., Schrage, D., & Kalev, A. (2015). Rage against the iron cage: The varied effects of bureaucratic personnel reforms on diversity. *American Sociological Review, 80*(5), 1014–1044. https://doi.org/10.1177/0003122415596416

Dobusch, L. (2021). The inclusivity of inclusion approaches: A relational perspective on inclusion and exclusion in organizations. *Gender, Work & Organization, 28*(1), 379–396. https://doi.org/10.1111/gwao.12574

Dover, T. L., Kaiser, C. R., & Major, B. (2020). Mixed signals: The unintended effects of diversity initiatives. *Social Issues and Policy Review, 14*(1), 152–181. https://doi.org/10.1111/sipr.12059

Eagly, A. H., & Carli, L. L. (2007). Women and the labyrinth of leadership. *Harvard Business Review, 85*(9), 63–71.

References

Eagly, A. H., & Koenig, A. M. (2021). The vicious cycle linking stereotypes and social roles. *Current Directions in Psychological Science, 30*(4), 343–350. https://doi.org/10.1177/09637214211013775

European Commission. (2020, September 18). *A union of equality: EU anti-racism action plan 2020–2025*. COM(2020) 565 final. Brussels. https://ec.europa.eu/info/sites/default/files/a_union_of_equality_eu_action_plan_against_racism_2020_-2025_en.pdf

Hassanzadeh, M., Silong, A. D., Asmuni, A., & Wahat, N. W. A. (2015). Developing effective global leadership. *Journal of Educational and Social Research, 5*(3), 161–168. https://doi.org/10.5901/jesr.2015.v5n3p15

Kramer, A. (2020). Recognizing workplace challenges faced by Black women leaders. *Forbes*. https://www.forbes.com/sites/andiekramer/2020/01/07/recognizing-workplace-challenges-faced-by-black-women-leaders/?sh=7b8a66e053e3

Lorde, A. (2021). The master's tools will never dismantle the master's house. In C. A. Schwartz (Ed.), *Twentieth-century literary criticism* (vol. 412). Gale. (Original work published 2007)

McCluney, C. L., et al. (2019, November 15). The costs of code-switching. *Harvard Business Review*. https://hbr.org/2019/11/the-costs-of-codeswitching

Nance-Nash, S. (2020, September 13). How corporate diversity initiatives trap workers of colour. BBC. https://www.bbc.com/worklife/article/20200826-how-corporate-diversity-initiatives-trap-workers-of-colour

Parker, P. S., & Ogilvie, D. T. (1996). Gender, culture, and leadership: Toward a culturally distinct model of African-American women executives' leadership strategies. *Leadership Quarterly, 7*(2), 189–214. https://doi.org/10.1016/S1048-9843(96)90040-5

Rosette, A. S., Koval, C. Z., Ma, A., & Livingston, R. (2016). Race matters for women leaders: Intersectional effects on agentic deficiencies and penalties. *The Leadership Quarterly, 27*(3), 429–445. https://doi.org/10.1016/j.leaqua.2016.01.008

Rosette, A. S., & Livingston, R. W. (2012). Failure is not an option for Black women: Effects of organizational performance on leaders with single versus dual-subordinate identities. *Journal of Experimental Social Psychology, 48*(5), 1162–1167. https://doi.org/10.1016/j.jesp.2012.05.002

Sanchez-Hucles, J. V., & Davis, D. D. (2010). Women and women of color in leadership: Complexity, identity, and intersectionality. *American Psychologist, 65*(3), 171–181. https://doi.org/10.1037/a0017459

Sanchez-Hucles, J., & Sanchez, P. (2007). From margin to center: The voices of diverse feminist leaders. In J. Chin, B. Lott, J. Rice & J. Sanchez-Hucles (Eds.), *Women and leadership: Transforming visions and diverse voices* (pp. 209–227). Malden, MA: Blackwell.

Shore, L. M., et al. (2011). Inclusion and diversity in work groups: A review and model for future research. *Journal of Management, 37*(4), 1262–1289. https://doi.org/10.1177/0149206310385943

Sweet, F. W. (2005). *Legal history of the color line: The rise and triumph of the one drop rule*. Backintyme.

Tackey, N. D., Tamkin, P., & Sheppard, E. (2001). *The problem of minority performance in organisations.* The Institute for Employment Studies. https://www.employment-studies.co.uk/system/files/resources/files/375.pdf

Tulshyan, R., & Burey, J-A. (2021, February 11). Stop telling women they have imposter syndrome. *Harvard Business Review.* https://hbr.org/2021/02/stop-telling-women-they-have-imposter-syndrome.

Wignot, J. (director) (2021). *Ailey.* [Film]. Goodhue Pictures, Inc.

Woods, D. R., Benschop, Y., & van den Brink, M. (2022). What is intersectional equality? A definition and goal of equality for organizations. *Gender Work & Organization, 29*(1), 92–109. https://doi.org/10.1111/gwao.12760.

Yukl, G. (2013). *Leadership in organizations* (8th ed.). Prentice Hall.

PART III: A MORE RADICAL ELSEWHERE
INTRODUCTION

Dillard, C. B. (2016). To address suffering that the majority can't see: Lessons from Black women's leadership in the workplace. *New Directions for Adult and Continuing Education, 2016*(152), 29–38.

Lara, A. M. (2020). *Queer freedom: Black sovereignty.* State University of New York Press.

Perlow, O. N., Wheeler, D. I., Bethea, S. L., & Scott, B. M. (Eds.). (2017). *Black women's liberatory pedagogies: Resistance, transformation, and healing within and beyond the academy.* Springer.

Taylor, S. R. (2021). *The body is not an apology: The power of radical self-love.* Berrett-Koehler Publishers.

CHAPTER 8: KEISHA VS. KAREN

Dumas, M. J. (2007). Sitting next to white children: School desegregation in the Black educational imagination (doctoral dissertation). City University of New York.

Epstein, R., Blake, J., & González, T. (2017). *Girlhood interrupted: The erasure of black girls' childhood.* Georgetown Law Center on Poverty and Inequality.

Freire, P. (2000). *Pedagogy of the oppressed* (30th anniversary ed.). Continuum.

Garcia, N. M., & Davila, E. R. (2021). Spirit murdering: Terrains, trenches, and terrors in academia: Introduction to special issue. *Educational Foundations, 34*(1).

Green, E. L. (2020, October 19). A battle for the souls of Black girls. *New York Times.*

Green, E. L., Walker, M., & Shapiro, E. (2020, October 2). Student discipline rates show Black girls are disproportionately at risk. *New York Times.*

Hardy, K. V. (2013). Healing the hidden wounds of racial trauma. *Reclaiming Children & Youth, 22*(1), 24–28.

Heywood, R. (2021). Racial trauma, language use and biases: A reflection on harmful practices in education. *Kieli, koulutus ja yhteiskunta, 12*(5). https://www.kieliverkosto.fi/fi/journals/kieli-koulutus-ja-yhteiskunta-lokakuu-2021/racial-trauma-language-use-and-biases-a-reflection-on-harmful-practices-in-education

Hines, D. E., & Wilmot, J. M. (2018). From spirit-murdering to spirit-healing: Addressing anti-Black aggressions and the inhumane discipline of Black children. *Multicultural Perspectives, 20*(2), 62–69.

Love, B. L. (2019). The "spirit murdering" of black and brown children. *Education Week, 38*(35), 18–19.

Morris, M. W. (2016). *Pushout: The criminalization of Black girls in schools*. The New Press.

National Center for Education Statistics. (2022). Characteristics of public school teachers. *Condition of Education*. US Department of Education, Institute of Education Sciences. https://nces.ed.gov/programs/coe/indicator/clr

CHAPTER 9: CONCLUSION

Dillard, C. B. (2016). To address suffering that the majority can't see: Lessons from Black women's leadership in the workplace. *New Directions for Adult and Continuing Education, 2016*(152), 29–38.

Garrett-Walker, W. L. (2021). Replanting a wild seed: Black women school leaders subverting ideological lynching. https://repository.usfca.edu/diss/567

Lara, A. M. (2020). *Queer freedom: Black sovereignty*. State University of New York Press.

Perlow, O. N., Wheeler, D. I., Bethea, S. L., & Scott, B. M. (Eds.). (2017). *Black women's liberatory pedagogies: Resistance, transformation, and healing within and beyond the academy*. Springer.

Taylor, S. R. (2021). *The body is not an apology: The power of radical self-love*. Berrett-Koehler Publishers.

Index

AAUW. *See* American Association of University Women
abundance thinking, 34
activism, leadership as, 90
Ade-Serrano, Yetunde, 95, 97, 99, 101
Africa, 8, 54
African warrior queens, 54, 57, 60–63
AfroBoriqua mothering, 18
Afrocentrism, 68
Afro-Futurism, 107
AfroLatinidad, 17, 21
AfroLatinx: Blackness and, 18, 33; feminisms, 17–18; leadership, 15–16, 22–25, 26–29, 35; mothering and, 16, 19–20
AfroPuerto Rican, 24
agency, 38, 50
aggression, 40
Agojie (all-female warriors), 54
ahijado (godchild), 19
Alameda County Public Health Department, 11
alcohol, 9, 10
Alexander, Sadie Mossell, 89
Allen, Gingi, 9, 11, 13
"all skin folk ain't kinfolk," 69
Amanirenas (African warrior queen), 54
American Association of University Women (AAUW), 89
American exceptionalism, 109

ancestral call, to midwifery, 8–9
Andean Indigenous communities, 19
Angelou, Maya, 27
"angry Black woman" stereotype, 53, 87, 99
anti-Blackness, 23, 76; chattel slavery system and, 75; dismantling, 110; female toxicity, 84; racism, 81
anti-racism, 81, 98–99
Aquino, Elena Aurora, 7
assistant midwives, 10–13
atrial fibrillation, 3, 4
audacity, 88
authentic leadership, 85
authentic selves, 102
autoethnography, Black feminist, 45–46
autonomy, 38, 39, 47

bachelor's degrees, 89
Bankole-Medina, K., 90
Barnett, Mary, 105
Bass, L., 90
becoming, process of, 29, 32
Bell, E. L. J., 67
belonging, sense of, 98
Bennett College, 90
Bethune, Mary McLeod, 53, 89
Bethune Cookman College, 89–90
biases, 48

BIPOC. *See* Black, Indigenous, People of Color
birthing traditions, 8–9
birth stories, 3–5; assistant midwife and, 10–13; becoming doula, 6–8
birth trauma, 3
birth work, 7
Black, Indigenous, People of Color (BIPOC), 6, 7, 42
Black borderlands, of Latinidad, 30
Black boys, 109
Black-centered leadership, 15, 19; AfroLatinx feminisms and, 17–18; conclusion, 35; discussion of, 29–35; mothering and, 18; process and positionality, 21–22; *testimonios* as methodology and method, 20–21; *testimonios* for, 22–29; theoretical grounding for, 16–17
Black educational imagination, 110
Black feminist autoethnography, 45–46
Black girls, 109
Black Lives Matter, 58, 80
Blackness, 16, 17, 23, 39, 41, 94; AfroLatinx and, 18, 33; learning of, 18; scripts of, 19; womanhood and, 46, 49. *See also* anti-Blackness
Black women. *See specific topics*
#BlackWomenAtWork, 48
Bland, Sandra, 41
bodyfeeding (breastfeeding), 4–5
boundaries, setting, 104, 117
boys, Black, 109
breastfeeding, 23, 28; as best practice, 34; bodyfeeding, 4–5; mother-child bonding through, 15
Brown, Brené, 70, 76
Brown University, 90
Burey, J-A., 102
Burke, M. G., 90

cafecito (coffee), 22
Cannonier, C., 90
cardiomyopathy, 3, 4

care: self-care, 61–62; in *testimonios*, 22–25
career self-efficacy, 92
Carli, L. L., 98
caste system, 68
CCT. *See* cultural contracts theory
Center for Hispanic Excellence: La Casa Latina, 21
Chance, N. L., 92
charlas (chats), 22
chattel slavery system, 75
Chisholm, Shirley, 62
"chocolate cities," 41
choice, 101
civil rights movement, 76
Clance, P. R., 100
Clifton, Lucille, 50
coalition, 62
code switching, 37, 101
co-fathers. *See compadres*
coffee. *See cafecito*
collaboration, 28
collective narrative, 42
Collins, Patricia Hill, 45, 53, 91
colonialism, 56
colonization, 8
Colored Women's League, 56
comadres (co-mothers), 19
community: Andean Indigenous, 19; COVID-19 and, 99; doula programs, 6; education and, 89; empowering, 31–32; strengthening, 16; transnational feminist praxis in, 20
community college students, 89
co-mothers. *See comadres*
compadres (co-fathers), 19
compassion, self-, 121
compassionate guidance, 32–33
compradazgo, 19
Conditions of Visibility (CoV), 47
conflict, 101
confusion, 43–44
consejos, 25
contractions, 3–4, 5, 11–12
Cookman Institute, 89

Index

Cortes, Krista L., 21, 30, 32
courage, in *testimonios*, 26–29
CoV. *See* Conditions of Visibility
COVID-19, 44, 99
Crenshaw, Kimberlé, 46, 96
Cruz, Celia, 24, 27
Cuba, 24
cultural backgrounds, 27
cultural contracts theory (CCT), 46–47
cultural invasion, 110

Dahomey (West African Kingdom), 54
daily practices, 17
dando LECHE (giving milk), 16, 29
Davila, E. R., 110
Davis, Viola, 54, 55
Daytona Beach Literary and Industrial School for Training Negro Girls, 89
decision-making, 122
DEIB. *See* Diversity, Equality, Inclusion, and Belonging
deities. *See* orisha/santos
Demerol, 4
depression: functional, 9; postpartum, 5
diasporic personhood, 32
Dillard, C. B., 68, 84, 90
Diversity, Equality, Inclusion, and Belonging, 42
Dominican Republic, 21
double jeopardy, 49
doulas, 6–8
Dumas, M. J., 110
Dykes, Eva, 89

Eagly, A. H., 98
Echavarria, E., 60, 62
education, 109–14; bachelor's degrees and, 89; Black educational imagination, 110. *See also* higher education
EFE. *See* endarkened feminist epistemology
Elder, C. C., 88, 94
emotional intelligence, 92
empowerment, 54; of communities, 31–32

endarkened feminist epistemology (EFE), 68
English as a second language (ESL), 26
Epps, S. K., 90
Epstein, R., 111
ESL. *See* English as a second language
Etalk (TV program), 55
exclusion, 43–44
expansive praxis, 34–35
expectations, of Black women, 38
expertise, of Black women, 44–49

fearlessness, 56
femininity, Black, 111
feminism, 68; AfroLatinx, 17–18; Black feminist autoethnography, 45–46; transnational feminist praxis, 20
fierceness, in *testimonios*, 22–25
fight-or-flight response, 38
Forbes (magazine), 87
Frasqueri, Destiny Nicole, 24
freedom, 60, 107; through love, 49–51
Friere, Paulo, 110
functional depression, 9

Garcia, N. M., 110
Garcia-Louis, C., 19
Gardner, L., 93
Garrett-Walker, Whitneé L., 65, 123–24
Gaudiano, Paolo, 87
gender, skin color and, 96–98
Georgetown Law Center on Poverty and Inequality, 111
Gervais, Roxane L., 95, 97, 100
girls, Black, 109
giving milk. *See dando LECHE*
glass-ceiling effect, 49
godchild. *See ahijado*
Gomes, Nazreen Ayo Dioni James, 13
grand midwives, 8, 13
Grant, Jacqueline, 61
Graser, Kristen, 9
guidance, compassionate, 32–33
Guzman, Roseilyn, 21, 30, 32

healing, seeking, 122
HEART model for Authentic Leadership, 85
Height, Dorothy, 56
high blood pressure, 120
higher education, 18, 89–90; *compradazgo* in, 19; as mothering, 15; Zeta Phi Beta, 24
Highland Hospital, 8
Hines, D. E., 110
Holder, A. M. B., 93
hooks, bell, 49, 63
Huang, B. L., 91
Hughes, C., 91, 92
"hush harbors," 74

ICU. *See* intensive care unit
identities, 27, 28, 94, 95; CCT and, 46–47; code switching and, 37; intersecting, 16, 18, 20, 32, 43, 56; markers of, 42; multiple, 55, 96; in work culture, 38
Imes, S. A., 100
imposter syndrome, 11, 99–101
inclusion, 98–99
Indigenous communities, Andean, 19
Indigenous knowledge, 30
individuality, 101
integrity, 115
intelligence, emotional, 92
intensive care unit (ICU), 4–5
interconnectedness, 19
internalized behavior, 40
"intersecting oppressions," 56
intersectionality, 46, 55, 96
"Invisible Army," 76

Jackson, Ketanji Brown, 67, 88
Jackson, M. A., 93
Jean-Marie, G., 48
"Jezebel" stereotype, 87, 111
Jim Crow, 75–76, 88
Jones, C., 67
justice: restorative, 118; social, 50

K-12 schooling, 110
Kanora, Karla, 15
Karen (stereotype), 111–14
Keisha (stereotype), 111–14
Kenny, C., 19
Keys, Alicia, 27
Kindred Soul Doula, 6
Knaus, C. B., 67
knowledge: centers of, 20; Indigenous, 30

labor, mother's milk and, 1
Lara, A. M., 17
Latinidad, 16, 17, 30
leadership. *See specific topics*
leche. *See* mother's milk
de Leon, Aya, 24
life stories, 20
Llanos-Figueroa, Dahlma, 24
Lorde, Audre, 53, 61, 102
love, 62–63; freedom through, 49–51; leading with, 30–31; self-love, 86
Love, Bettina, 110
"Love Is the Practice of Freedom" (hooks), 63
Lukumi traditions, 25

"The Majestic Place" (Garrett-Walker), 123–24
MALA MADRE, 18
"Mammy" stereotype, 53, 87, 111
Mariposa, 24
Martin, Trayvon, 76
McCluney, C. L., 47
McEwen, B. S., 61
microaggressions, 43, 55, 79, 93, 111
micro-insults, 55
micro-invalidations, 55
midwives and midwifery: ancestral call to, 8–9; assistant, 10–13
Midwives of Color (blog), 6
milk. *See dando LECHE;* mother's milk
Moraga, Cherrie, 32
mothering, 32; AfroBoriqua mothering, 18; AfroLatinx and, 16,

19–20; higher education as, 15; understanding of, 28
mother's milk, 1, 15, 22–23
Muhammad, K. G., 76
Mullen, C. A., 67
"My Intentions as a Birthworker" (journal entry), 8

Nanny (African warrior queen), 54
National Association of Colored Women, 56
National Center for Education Statistics, 109
National Federation of Afro-American Women, 56
negotiation, 46
Nkomo, S., 67
norms, societal, 18
"Now I Lay Me Down: Rest as Resistance" (Clifton), 50
Nyong'o, Lupita, 54
Nzinga (African warrior queen), 54

Olayiwola, Porsha, 63
oral history, 20
orisha/santos (deities), 25
othering, 37

Pachamama, 19
pain medication, 4
panic, 38
Pastrana, Fermina Gómez, 24
personhood, diasporic, 32
pigmentation, 23
Pitocin, 4
Player, Willa, 90
"playing the game," 39
"playing the race card," 81
Ponterro, J. G., 93
postpartum depression, 5
power minimization, of selves, 104
praxis, expansive and transformative, 34–35
preeclampsia, 120
pregnancy, 3–6, 118–20

Prince George's County, Maryland, 41
PTSD, 121
Puerto Rico, 24

Quaye, S. J., 61
queens, African warrior, 54, 57, 60–63

Rabelo, V. C., 47, 48
racial oppression, 110
racism, 48–49, 53, 60, 63, 74, 78, 88, 90; anti-Black, 81; anti-racism, 81, 98–99; global consciousness around, 58
radical resistance, *48*, 49–51
reciprocity, 19
refueling, 60–63
re-memorialization, 54
remote work, 44
replenishment, 62
resilience, 74; in *testimonios*, 26–29
resistance, structures of, 43
rest, 37–38
restorative justice, 118
Reyes-Barriéntez, A., 19
RLBC. *See* Roots of Labor Birth Collective
Robertson, K., 67
Rogers-Ard, R., 67, 84, 85
Roots of Labor Birth Collective (RLBC), 7

Sales, S., 90
Sanchez, Victoria, 24
Santería, 24, 25, 32
"Sapphire" stereotype, 111
Sardeshmukh, Anjali, 13
Scary Spice (Spice Girls member), 24
Seales, Amanda, 71
self-affirmations, 62
self-authorship, 93
self-care, 61–62
self-compassion, 121
self-definition, 56–60, 91, 101
self-doubt, 32, 78
self-efficacy, 92

self-evaluation, 91
self-image, 100
self-love, 86
self-preservation, 61–62
self-worth, 83
sexism, 48, 49, 53, 63, 88, 90
Shorter-Gooden, K., 67
silence, 43–44
Simmons, Ruth, 90
Simpson, Georgiana, 89
skin color, gender and, 96–98
skin-to-skin contact, 15
slavery, 74, 76–77, 88, 111; chattel slavery system, 75; trade, 54
Smith, S. M., 62
social justice, 50
social practice, mothering as, 15
societal norms, 18
sorority, Black, 24
Sparks, Jordin, 27
Spice Girls, 24
spirit murdering, 110
Stellar, E., 61
stereotypes, 48, 59, 96–97; "angry Black woman," 53, 87, 99; "Jezebel," 87, 111; Karen, 111–14; Keisha, 111–14; "Mammy," 53, 87, 111; "Sapphire," 111; "welfare mother/queen," 53, 87
support system, 103–4
suppression, of Black women, 45
Supreme Court, US, 88

teachers, White, 109–10
Terrell, Mary Church, 56
testimoniando, 20, 35
testimonios, 16, 30–32, 35; courage and resilience in, 26–29; fierceness and care in, 22–25; as methodology and method, 20–21; "theory in the flesh" and, 33
"theory in the flesh," 32, 33
Third-World knowledge, 20
39-week appointment, 5
Thompkins, T., 67
transformative praxis, 34–35
transnational feminist praxis, 20
trauma, birth, 3

Trump, Donald, 88
trust, of selves, 104
truth, telling one's, 20
Turtle Island, 8
Twitter (X), 48
typecasting, 53

University of Pennsylvania, 21
upskilling, of others, 104
US Supreme Court, 88

Vega, Marta Moreno, 24

Walker, Jayland, 76
warrior queens, African, 54, 57, 60–63
Washing Society, 56
"welfare mother/queen" stereotype, 53, 87
West Africa, 54
White-dominant organizations, 39
White fragility, 43
White gaze, 48
Whiteness, 38, 39, 48, 68, 110
White supremacy, 43, 50, 72–73, 76, 78
White teachers, 109–10
White women, 71
"Why Black Women Are Better Leaders" (Gaudiano), 87
Wilkerson, I., 76
Williams, O., 60, 62
Wilmot, J. M., 110
womanhood, 46, 49, 53, 55, 94
The Woman King (film), 54–55, 63
"A Woman Will Manifest" (Garrett-Walker), 65
women. *See specific topics*
Woods, D. R., 104
work culture, 38

X. *See* Twitter

Yoruba people, 25
young adults, 7
youth development, 7

Zeta Phi Beta (Black sorority), 24
Zoom, 11

About the Contributors

EDITORS

Wendi Williams. Psychologist, advocate, and educator, Dr. Wendi Williams applies her work at the intersection of education and psychology to her scholarship and leadership praxis. Williams completed undergraduate studies at the University of California, Davis, where she majored in psychology and minored in African and African American Studies. She completed graduate study at Pepperdine University (MA in psychology) and Georgia State University, where she earned a doctorate in counseling psychology, with an emphasis in multicultural psychology and family systems. Williams began her career as assistant professor in counselor education at Long Island University—Brooklyn and has served as an academic administrator for progressive, justice-focused higher education institutions like Bank Street College of Education and Mills College, School of Education. She joined Fielding Graduate University as provost and senior vice president in October 2022. Dr. Williams is an accomplished scholar in the areas of Black women and girls leadership and development, most notably with her recently published book, *Black Women at Work: On Refusal and Recovery*. Learn more about Dr. Williams's work at drwendiwilliams.com.

Dr. Whitneé L. Garrett-Walker (she/her) is the Assistant Dean of Credentialing and Partnerships in the School of Education, University of San Francisco. Whitneé is a Black, Indigenous (Natchitoches Tribe of Louisiana, enrolled member), and Queer wife, mother, and scholar born and raised on Raymaytush Ohlone Land. She earned a BA in history from UC Berkeley, a master's degree in teaching from Saint Mary's College of California, and an EdD from the University of San Francisco. She has extensive experience loving, living, and working in the field of public education and has spent over a decade as a middle and high school teacher, instructional coach, and school administrator in urban public schools in Oakland Unified and San Francisco Unified School Districts, respectively. Dr. Garrett-Walker is a triple-credentialed California educator who believes deeply in the power of critical hope, healing, and educational justice in the field of education. As a scholar practitioner, she uses qualitative research as the foundation of feeding her desire to *explore and make known* the experiences of the promise, challenge, and potential of Black and Indigenous women in educational leadership.

ASSOCIATE EDITOR

Nia Spooner is a former educator and current doctoral student in educational leadership and policy at the Ontario Institute for Studies in Education, University of Toronto. Nia earned her BA in education from Smith College and her MEd from the University of Toronto. She is passionate about education and has extensive experience teaching in cross-cultural contexts. After completing her teaching practicum in Massachusetts, Nia was awarded a Fulbright Scholarship, which brought her teaching career to Taiwan for one year. She further developed her teaching and language skills as a middle and high school educator in Shanghai. All of her education, teaching, and lived experiences as a Black and Chinese woman have informed her scholarly interests. Nia's research focuses on culturally responsive and equity-oriented leadership in education.

CONTRIBUTORS

Dr. Yetunde Ade-Serrano is a BPS chartered counseling psychologist and an HCPC registered practitioner psychologist who has been in the field of psychotherapy for more than two decades. She is the co-founder of Black and Asian Counseling Psychologists' Group and the past chair of the BPS Division of Counseling Psychology. She is primarily in independent practice and has additional clinical experience within the National Health Service, Voluntary Sectors, Prison Service, to name a few. She is a mentor, visiting lecturer, and an external examiner on DPsych training programs, as well as a clinical supervisor. Her clinical interests include self-exploration and growth, Black women's identity, African psychology and spirituality, how individuals and communities make meaning, and working with race and difference across cultures.

Norka Blackman-Richards is a curator of anti-racist equity-needing spaces and movements. This work is aligned with more than two decades supporting student success in higher education for the City University of New York. Norka lectures in literature composition and is the director of the Percy E Sutton SEEK Program at Queens College, one of the oldest opportunity programs in the United States. Educated under the British, Dutch, and Latin American educational systems, Norka has a deep respect for diversity of cultures, customs, and people. A nonprofit leader, direct descendant of the builders of the Panama Canal, and the daughter of missionaries, Norka acknowledges how the intersections of her lived experiences and identities are ever-present in her many roles in and outside academia.

Krista L. Cortes, PhD (she/they), is a first-generation AfroPuerto Rican mother/scholar/activist, raised in the diaspora. As an academic and administrator, Cortes focuses on transformative research and practices aimed at uplifting historically oppressed and marginalized individuals within university settings. Cortes's published works delve into the intricacies of how Blackness permeates various practices within AfroLatinx communities, with a specificity of how Blackness is taught and learned as a lived [AfroLatinx] experience. Presently, Cortes holds the position of director of the Center for Hispanic Excellence—La Casa Latina at the University of Pennsylvania.

Andrea E. Evans, PhD, recently retired as the interim provost and vice president of Academic Affairs at Northeastern Illinois University (Chicago). Previously she served as interim dean of the Goodwin College of Education and as director of the Carruthers Center for Inner City Studies at NEIU. Prior to going to NEIU, Dr. Evans served as dean of the College of Education at Governors State University and as an administrator and/or professor at Southern Illinois University Carbondale, Northern Illinois University, and University of Illinois Chicago. She is a published scholar in educational leadership and policy, diversity, and equity. Prior to working in higher education, Dr. Evans was a high school science teacher and principal of an alternative high school in the Chicago area. Dr. Evans completed her PhD in education policy studies and BS in biological sciences at the University of Illinois Chicago and her MEd in curriculum and program development at DePaul University. In 2020 Dr. Evans was appointed by Governor Pritzker to serve a 6-year term as a member of the Illinois Board of Higher Education.

Dr. Roxane L. Gervais is a registered occupational psychologist, independent practitioner, consultant, coach, and mentor. Her extensive experience in her field allows her to provide various services, including developing and facilitating training on organizational leadership, work-related stress, and work-relevant mental health to support workers and organizations. She uses her expertise to address those occupational safety and health issues that arise, allowing her to apply an evidenced-based approach, such as conducting stress audits within organizations, to promote safe and healthy practices and enhance work conditions. Her professional and research interests cover the work environment through assessing the well-being of individuals, inclusive of job stress and strain, mental health, job satisfaction, work-life balance, behavior change, communication, flexible working, organizational change, and diversity, inclusive of gender, generational issues, and the life course. Widely published, she is an invited speaker at conferences, leads projects internationally, and works across sectors and industries.

Roseilyn Guzman is a mama, sister, *hermana*, *titi*, daughter, and friend. Roseilyn is strong and kind, happy and resilient. She has chosen to occupy this space with the pride of the story that follows her family's history. She focuses on providing a grounding space for each person to come as they are, beautifully and uniquely created, in the hopes that she will understand their story and passions—all while giving herself the room to grow and develop each day. For Roseilyn, leadership is extending her hand to lift as she climbs and/or walk beside her sisters and brothers. It is a relationship in which grace and compassion take precedence as she works through the expectations and systems she has been forced to operate in. She occupies this space as an AfroLatina woman who chooses to celebrate *su latinidad* and identities to create the spaces for others to thrive and work toward the best versions of themselves.

Dr. Renée Heywood began her career in education almost 30 years ago as a foreign language teacher in public, private, and graduate school settings. She is recognized for her leadership in juvenile justice education. Her work on bias in language education was recognized at the Language Education for Social Justice Conference in Jyvaskyla, Finland, resulting in an international publication titled *Racial Trauma, Language Use and Biases: A Reflection on Harmful Practices in Education.* She has a PhD in teacher education and curriculum studies at the University of Massachusetts Amherst, with a focus on language, literacy, and culture. Her latest book is titled *Finding Me Finding Us for Educators: A Reflection Journal for Racial Reconciliation.* Renée has traveled the world to support education and youth development in Guatemala, Nicaragua, and Australia and has presented her work on racism in education at multiple venues. She is an assistant superintendent of Equity, Diversity, and Inclusion at one of the largest school districts in New England and is the CEO/founder of her own consulting company, Real Talk Leadership (RealTalkLeadership.com).

About the Contributors

Rhema Heywood is a singer/songwriter who is establishing herself in the music industry as a published recording artist. She has been singing and dancing since the age of 4 and began songwriting at the age of 10. Her career in the performing arts has won international recognition, and she has performed at venues throughout New England and Hollywood, such as the Hard Rock Cafe and First Night Boston New Year's Eve televised show. She is currently working on her gifts of poetry and song and is making her mark as a strong leader for this generation as one of the youngest members of the Real Talk Leadership staff.

Dr. Rachelle Rogers-Ard is a published author and organizational development specialist with more than 25 years' experience preparing adults to disrupt racist policies, practices, and procedures that threaten organizational health. Dr. Rogers-Ard is the principal lead for Harvest Consulting, where she designs and facilitates customized leadership training utilizing social-emotional best practices. As a certified Dare to Lead and The Leadership Challenge trainer, Rachelle's work showcases the necessity for organizational core values to drive employee retention and improve team outcomes. Dr. Rogers-Ard challenges leaders to interrogate systemic racism if they are to effectively lead across difference; her own Authentic Leadership framework provides guiding questions for personal reflection toward inclusive organizational development. Her latest publication, "Critical Race Teacher Leadership: Leading Anti-racist Systems Change," highlights her "Five Ds" framework for transformative disruption. Dr. Rogers-Ard is also the founder, content developer, and facilitator for Black Women: Life, Love, and Leadership (BW3L), an unapologetic affinity space for Black folx to share and develop strategies that combat racial oppression.

Kaiayo Zitkála Shatteen (they/them/theirs) is an Afro Indigenous (Aniyunwiya & Chahta), Queer parent of two young adults. They live on the Unceded Land of the Lisjan Ohlone People, where they are a reproductive justice advocate, apprentice midwife, LGBTQIA2S+ equity consultant, and a recovery motivational speaker. They give thanks to their ancestors for guiding them daily. Kaiayo has a deep commitment to ending the injustice that puts BIPOC and LGBTQIA2S+ and gender nonconforming communities at the bottom when it comes to positive birth outcomes, access to inclusive and traditional healthcare, and equity in the workplace. They are a practicing Buddhist, holding the Five Precepts and the Eightfold Path near their heart. Kaiayo shares the benefits of their sobriety and the joys of staying on the path of recovery. They are open, free, and live courageously with love, joy, and compassion. Kaiayo is a midwifery student in their last year of school and will be starting a homebirth midwifery practice in Huichin/

Oakland, California, once they are licensed as a certified professional midwife.

DeLisha Tapscott, EdD, is a leadership educator and social change agent who amplifies the voices of Black women in various spaces and platforms. She holds a doctor of education degree in leadership for organizations from the University of Dayton, where she examined the intersectional experiences of identity negotiation and Black women within White-dominant spaces. As a facilitator, writer, and founder of BSW Chronicles, an online community space for Black women, she has spoken and written about social justice, the experiences of Black women within society, and intersectionality at various venues, such as Harvard University, Texas A&M University, and the University of Maryland.

www.ingramcontent.com/pod-product-compliance
Lightning Source LLC
Chambersburg PA
CBHW051118230426
43667CB00014B/2638